The *Rational* Nationalist

RealClear
Publishing

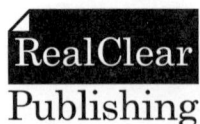

www.amplifypublishinggroup.com
www.realclearpublishing.com

The Rational Nationalist: Moving Beyond Partisanship Toward Prosperity

For more information, please contact:
RealClear Publishing, an imprint of Amplify Publishing Group
620 Herndon Parkway, Suite 220
Herndon, VA 20170
info@amplifypublishing.com

Library of Congress Control Number: 2025912425

CPSIA Code: PRV1025A

ISBN-13: 979-8-89138-783-6

Printed in the United States

The *Rational* Nationalist

Moving Beyond *Partisanship* Toward *Prosperity*

LEE ELLIS

RealClear
Publishing

CONTENTS

Part I: Philosophical Framework

Part II: Historical and Political Analysis

PART I

Philosophical Framework

This book sets out to provide a new prism through which to approach the political world and public policy—one that can help us overcome our divisions and keep our focus on strengthening our nation. We will begin by examining the building blocks of this philosophy—its views on the state of nature, morality, the law, and the role of the individual within society. We will then use what we have discussed to examine human history and political relations. In this section, the focus will be on British and American history, examining the factors that allowed Britain and the United States to become global powers, and how the lessons learned from this history can be used to better formulate public policy. I call this approach to politics "Rational Nationalism."

In writing about Rational Nationalism, one must start by defining exactly what is meant by this term. "Nationalism" is devotion and dedication to one's nation and the prioritization of the national good over one's individual self-interest. "Rational" refers to the use of our intellect, using logical reasoning and empirical data rather than our emotions to make decisions.

Rational Nationalism, then, is loyalty to the well-being of the nation, the prioritization of national interests over partisan or personal interests, and the willingness to put aside emotional reactions in favor of a deliberative evidence-based decision-making process. It involves the willingness to put aside our differences so we can work together to achieve common goals—even when we have different opinions on how to best achieve those goals. It is support for practical, pragmatic solutions over those driven by ideology. Most importantly, it is putting the well-being of the group over the well-being of the individual.

The need for a group-driven philosophy, for the individual to focus on the good of the nation instead of individual or partisan interests, is now stronger than ever. We are a nation divided against itself, where an alarming number of people view as their primary enemy not foreign powers or terrorists, but other Americans. We have consistently seen our leaders put their egos and ideologies above the well-being of the nation, opting to ratchet up division and partisanship in a pathetic attempt to win a game of political football rather than lead with the policies needed to restore America to its rightful place atop the international food chain.

We've become a generation that believes in nothing. Too often our young people like to think of themselves as too smart to believe in anything greater than themselves. They worship at the altar of faux intellectualism, disparaging ideas such as patriotism and morality to prove their supposed intellectual mettle. They reject devotion to their nation in favor of devotion to "humanity," rallying around the popular cause du jour, though their activism rarely amounts to more than posting a couple of pictures and crying some very public crocodile tears.

Throughout history, people have understood the fundamental importance of standing up and sacrificing for the well-being of their family and their nation. To do so is a basic human instinct. As a nation, we have become so obsessed with the individual's ego and sense of grievance that we ignore this very basic human instinct. It's time our generation puts aside our pride and sense of entitlement to stand for something greater than ourselves. It's time to stand for our nation.

CHAPTER 1

The State of Nature

Let's begin our discussion with the most basic building block of any philosophy: the state of nature. What was the individual like in the state of nature, and how does that differ from modern man? How did he interact with others compared to modern society? The answers have been pondered by great thinkers like Locke, Rousseau, and Hobbes, and no consensus has emerged. Theories have ranged from an ordered, efficient quasi-society to savage chaos. Modern research can provide some insights, though there remains a great deal of debate and uncertainty.

To state what should be obvious: on an individual, biological basis, modern man is no different from natural man. Evolution takes hundreds of thousands of years to occur, and we have been civilized for only around ten thousand. Even then, most of those years of "civilization" were spent in primitive societies that fall far short of what we would term "civilization" today. Though there may be significant differences due to socialization and living conditions, modern man is a creature molded by an evolution that occurred in a pre-civilization environment. Modern man suffers many problems today because we're essentially cavemen living in the modern world, and this fact can provide insight into how to address these problems.

Many of the behaviors, instincts, and traits that led us to thrive in the "state of nature" are counterproductive in modern society. We evolved at a time when humans lived in small bands of mostly direct or extended families, and anyone outside the band was a threat. Today, we live in multicultural cities consisting of thousands, if not millions, of unrelated people. We encounter strangers on a daily basis, very few of whom pose any threat to our well-being. The instincts we evolved to protect ourselves and thrive to survive wild animals and competition from other tribes do not necessarily translate into our modern lifestyle.

That being said, it would be a mistake to assume that we are no longer in a state of nature simply because of the dramatic differences in our day-to-day lives. The defining feature of a state of nature is that we are free to do whatever we want, whenever we want. Our only limitations are our physical limitations. However, within the realm of possibility, we are as free to choose any course of action today as we ever were. The only thing that's changed is how other people react to what we do.

The fundamental error that people make in arguing that we have left the state of nature into a different, civilized state is that there is now a society to regulate and curtail our range of action through laws and punishment. However, what is overlooked is that if we are free to act as we wish, then everyone else possesses this same freedom of action. In other words, I am still as free to steal from you or attack you as I ever was. The fact that we now have a police force that will arrest and punish me for doing so hasn't curtailed my ability to do so. It has merely altered the external consequences of choosing that course of action. Though I can attack you as easily as ever, I now have a better idea of how others will respond. While this may appear on its surface to have removed us from the state of nature, it has not. The error in this thinking is simplifying the transaction of my assault on you into a transaction between just us.

The related objection would be that absent a social or other incentive to do so, other people are unlikely to intervene on behalf of the victim in a state of nature, whereas in society this is almost certain to occur. Again, this is wrong. It is very likely that, in a state of nature, at the very least, the family or friends of the victim are likely to seek some sort of revenge. The victim may even appeal to unrelated individuals, at least some of whom would be likely to assist out of some innate sense of justice. Even if you reject the notion that some people would act out of a sense of right and wrong and believe that all humans only act out of rational self-interest, it is still likely that others would band together to punish the aggressor. After all, if I am willing to attack you, it is likely I would be willing to attack anyone else weaker than I am, and therefore it is in everyone's self-interest to band together to prevent me from doing so.

Nevertheless, although we are as free to act today as we have been at any point in history, there is no doubt that we act differently in a modern society than we would in a tribal society, or a medieval society for that matter. This is because other individuals have changed the perceived consequences of our actions, thus changing the equation of our mental calculations and the decisions we reach from them. Though the evolution of human society from prehistoric times to the present has not curtailed human freedom, it has changed the environment in which we exercise this freedom. Freedom to act is not freedom to act without consequences, and the two main ways in which those consequences manifest in society are law and morality.

CHAPTER 2

Constraints on Human Behavior

Though nothing about society removes us outright from a state of nature, civilization undeniably constrains human behavior. Society primarily achieves this through two mechanisms: law and morality. These systems punish individuals who violate societal rules and teach them to internalize values that benefit the collective. When these are effectively applied, they can synergize to guide individuals toward actions that optimally benefit society.

LAW

The most obvious and simplest way in which societies encourage their members to behave in a way that benefits the society is through the law. Although the law has evolved to encompass a complicated web of principles, precedents, and procedures, it is at its core the use or threat of force to promote behavior that society wishes to encourage, or, more often, to discourage behavior deemed harmful to society. This is accomplished by declaring beforehand how society will respond should an individual act in certain ways. For example, throughout history, it has generally been the case that if you kill someone, then other members of that society will kill you.

The law is simply an overt declaration of how others will respond to certain behaviors of an individual in an attempt to get people to behave or not behave in certain ways. If you steal a loaf of bread, I will cut off your hand. It's a threat others were always free to make, and one they may or may not follow through on should you decide to steal the bread anyway. After all, some crimes go unpunished due to apathy, corruption, or ambiguity. Any individual is as free as they ever were to steal bread but is now (arguably) less likely to do so because the intended reactions of others have been made clear.

If law is nothing more than the predeclared use of force to encourage some behaviors and discourage others, then when exactly does law become law? In clan societies, no doubt members had a pretty good idea of the consequences for harming other members of the clan and for certain other actions. Sometimes, these consequences may even have been explicitly spelled out, and yet we would be hard-pressed to consider members of the clan ostracizing or eliminating offending members in an ad hoc manner "law." The premeditated use of force to respond to certain actions or inactions of members of a group can properly be called law when it is codified and consistent in its application.

Consistent application of the law does not necessarily mean equality before the law. Some of the earliest examples of codified laws, such as Hammurabi's Code, doled out dramatically different punishments depending on the places of the accused and the victim in the social hierarchy. Nor does it necessarily mean that enforcement is consistent, as can be seen to this day in places that struggle with police corruption. All it means is that what is considered a crime today will be considered a crime tomorrow.

When humans lived in small clans, it was sufficient for disputes and transgressions to be dealt with by the clan on an ad hoc basis. However, as humans settled from nomadic hunter-gatherers into more complex agrarian societies, codified law became a necessity. It's difficult to motivate someone to spend months working the land to yield a crop that can be easily taken from them, so societies had to guarantee that their labor would be rewarded. Furthermore, interactions with strangers became more frequent, and so a standardized code of conduct was necessary, along with recourse should anyone violate this code. This necessity of predictability allowed societies to function and gave us the first source of codified laws.

In the Anglosphere, this has taken the form of English common law, a complex system of laws that has evolved over almost a thousand years. This started in the early days, with judges deciding cases in England following the Norman Conquest. As time went on, judges followed their own previous rulings as well as the rulings of other judges, and a series of principles and precedents developed that guided judicial rulings and gave them a sense of legitimacy and predictability. These principles and precedents became the common law, and the fact that judges, at least in theory, follow the law rather than their own sense of justice or personal preference is what gives the law predictability and stability.

Today, many of these common law principles have been codified into statutory law, and those that haven't continue to rule in lieu of a statute to the contrary. More importantly, this idea of precedent and judicial interpretation has been applied to statutes as well, as the statutes passed by legislative bodies are interpreted and applied to specific cases. Nowhere can this be seen more clearly than in the body of case law surrounding the United States Constitution, particularly the parts concerning the rights of American citizens. The common law, along with the accompanying principles, rights, and protections, is one of the greatest accomplishments of English society, if not the greatest, giving citizens of the Anglosphere justice, predictability, and the protection of their basic rights.

The rule of law and the guarantee of certain rights to the individual give the concept of law in English-speaking countries an aura of legitimacy. Legitimacy is the soft power exercised by the law. In contrast to hard power, such as the threat of a prison sentence or enforcement by police officers using force, soft power is the ability to persuade people to behave in a certain manner, not because they fear any repercussions or hope for any reward, but because they feel it is consistent with their own innate sense of justice. Because the law is viewed in English-speaking countries as just and its citizens feel protected by it, many will follow the law even in instances where they could break it with impunity. Thus, the law takes on an almost mystical quality in the minds of many, transforming from a mere set of rules to avoid punishment into a basic moral duty.

Anglo-American jurisprudence is such a complex web of procedures, regulations, and precedents that it is sometimes easy to forget what the law really is. For all its rights, procedural protections, and the great esteem in which we hold the law, at the end of the day it is still the use of previously agreed upon force to promote compliance among members of society. True, the majority of people may comply with a court order or a ruling because of the legitimacy bestowed upon the courts as fair arbiters, or because they recognize that this peaceful system of dispute resolution will benefit them in the long run, even if they are on the losing end today. However, to see that the power of the law still has its foundation in the use of force, let's explore exactly how the courts enforce their rulings.

If someone refuses to comply with a court order, they will be held in contempt of court. In other words, your options are to comply with the court or be seized and thrown in jail by law enforcement officers acting on the court's behalf. Somebody refusing to pay a civil reward or fine may have their property seized and sold by the sheriff. In any instance, it is the use of force or threat thereof that coerces compliance from unwilling members of society. Of course, all this depends on the fact that the majority of society will listen to the court, either out of respect for the legitimacy of the law, or because they recognize that they, their families, and society at large will benefit from the stability and predictability that respect for the law provides. If there were a widespread willingness to disregard the law as interpreted and enforced by the courts, the judicial system would cease to function, and court rulings would become meaningless. All it would take for the American judicial system to break down is for a bailiff to say "no."

Because the law deals with modifying incentives to encourage human beings to behave in a way that is conducive to the efficient functioning of society, there is a need for the law to be pragmatic. Laws must be made with an eye toward the reality of what people are, rather than the ideal of what we would like them to be. Human beings are nothing more than really intelligent animals, and their motivations are driven primarily by their base animal instincts. Even the intelligence people possess is nothing more than an evolutionary tool to help humans satisfy their animalistic desires. Though it is possible for people to rise above their primitive nature, the law must recognize that most people are going to pursue their own base instincts, regardless of what the law says about it. Thus, rather than trying to legislate people into behaving in an ideal way that would optimize the benefit to society, it is necessary to use the law pragmatically, containing these primitive drives the best we can and minimizing the externalities and harm to society that they cause. Laws should not be written to demand the behavior we would like people to exhibit; rather, they should be written with a recognition of how people will behave in response to the law.

For example, drug policy should not necessarily make it illegal to do drugs, even if this would be our ideal outcome. Rather, it should be written to minimize the damage drugs do to society at large, knowing that some people will pursue drugs regardless of their legality. We must recognize when we pass laws that a certain percentage of society will either ignore the law outright, attempt to find a way around the law, or attempt to find a way to engage in the banned behavior, violating the spirit and intent of the law while complying with the letter of the law. This isn't to say that simply banning the undesirable activity is always the wrong approach, and it certainly is not to say that we should ever tolerate or accept violations of the law. It is simply to recognize that the law is based on the use of hard power, i.e., force, to modify behavior, and as such is limited in its efficacy.

MORALITY

Just because the hard power of the law is limited in its ability to control human behavior does not mean that society must accept less than ideal behavior on the part of its citizens. Human behavior can also be modified by the exercise of soft power in the form of morality. Social morals can impact individuals' behavior through either extrinsic motivation, such as social expectations, pressures, and rewards, or intrinsic motivation, where the individual has internalized society's morality and acts accordingly. In either case, people will act in the manner most beneficial to the group, even if it goes against their own self-interest, and even though they are not being forced to do so. It is interesting to note, however, that at times, the extrinsic factors can be intense enough to more closely resemble hard power than soft.

Throughout most of human history, there was no distinction between legality and morality. Take the Ten Commandments, for instance. In addition to being one of the earliest law codes, they form the basis of Judeo-Christian morality. To this day, many Islamic countries incorporate Sharia law into their judicial practices, deriving their laws from the teachings of the Quran. It is a relatively recent development, inspired by increased secularism, to separate law and morality. To this day, even in the United States, the two often remain intertwined. Forcing one's moral beliefs onto others seems to be an instinctive human impulse.

The primary distinction between morality and legality is the source of the motivation to act in a way that is in society's interest. The motivation to follow the law is external, i.e., it comes from fear of punishment from an outside source, as discussed above. Morality, by contrast, has an internal motivation. People behave in a way that is consistent with their morals because they believe it is the right thing to do and are intrinsically motivated to do so. People are not coerced to behave morally unless the moral code they are violating also violates a legal code. There are no hard consequences for behaving immorally, though there may be soft repercussions (such as ostracism, scorn, or the distrust of others), particularly where an individual has the reputation of consistently behaving in a way deemed morally unacceptable.

The advantage of morality, from the group's perspective, is that it can impact behaviors in ways that the law cannot. First, if morality has been internalized, then the individual will behave morally even when no one is looking, since the motivation to do so comes from one's own conscience. Second, morality can impact human behavior in areas where legal regulation may be inefficient or ineffective. Individuals volunteer their time and give money to charity, both of which benefit the social group at the expense of said individual, not because they are legally required to do so, but because they think it is the right thing to do. In some areas, morality leads to individuals refraining from activity harmful to society more effectively than the law does. Though I won't go into detail here, I would argue that legal regulations regarding drug use and sexual behavior are, by and large, ineffective. However, many people will regulate their own behavior to be less harmful to society if they feel a moral calling to do so.

Where, then, does morality come from? Is morality hardwired within our genome, or is it nothing more than a social construct? Clearly, some morality derives from religion and social norms, but to what extent is religion the source of morality, and to what extent are religions merely the codification of existing moral codes and their attribution to a source greater than man? Most importantly, is morality absolute, with some things being definitively right or wrong? Or is it relative, varying from culture to culture and individual to individual, and purely subjective, with nothing being right or wrong except for in the mind of the individual judging the situation?

Religion gives a nice, clean answer to this question. Morality is absolute, because there is some form of higher being or higher universal order, and this determines what is right or wrong. Furthermore, this absolute form of morality can be discovered and known by man, either through scripture, prayer, or some other means taught by the religion. Some things are right, others are wrong, and God decides. However, in the absence of any sort of religious belief, or at least a degree of agnosticism, how are we mere mortals to decide which is which? Can absolute morality exist without an ultimate arbiter to decide what is right and what is wrong, or does secular thought necessitate a commitment to moral relativism?

Though by no means do I intend to resolve the debate here, for my part, I lean ever so slightly toward moral relativism. Clearly, there are differences in moral perceptions from culture to culture, as is evident in cultural attitudes toward sexuality, abortion, and capital punishment. It's not even as simple as saying that cultural differences exist with regards to morality, as these differences can be observed within a single culture. Americans, even Americans with a significantly similar environment, education, and background, have incredibly different views regarding the morality of certain actions. In the absence of some neutral, moral arbiter, how are we to determine which of the varying views is the correct one? It seems hubristic to think that, out of over eight billion people on this planet, only you possess moral clarity. Why, then, should we value our own moral judgment over that of anyone else? I would go so far as to argue that there is no right or wrong, nothing is moral or immoral, and actions "just are" until some observer labels them and attaches a moral judgment. Even then, the morality or immorality of the situation is simply in the eye of the beholder, having no meaning or authority to anyone else. In the words of the third umpire from an old baseball joke,[1] some are balls, some are strikes, but they ain't nothing until you call them.

And yet, there is something alluring about moral absolutism that makes it difficult to deny. It's easy to hem and haw at the margins, picking out the most controversial, difficult issues, pointing out that people disagree, and attempting to use this to demonstrate the meaninglessness of morality, but such an approach seems overly detached, intellectual, and off the mark. The vast majority of our lives are not lived in a moral gray area. We may argue about when killing is justified, but nobody, save a few sociopaths, is going to deny that unjustified killing is wrong. We all agree stealing is wrong, though we can have philosophical debates about when, if ever, it's justified. The common threads of morality can be found in most, if not all, major religious traditions, and seem to be hardwired and instinctual. In fact, I would argue that most of the time people struggle less with knowing what the right thing to do is and more with finding the courage to do it. Exploring the gray areas of morality may make for some interesting intellectual debates, but it is, for the most part, removed from the everyday practice of morality, where most situations have a clear right and wrong.

This leads us to wonder exactly what constitutes a moral gray area. Is it simply majority rule? This doesn't seem right, as even in the grayest of areas there will be a majority decision, unless there are more than two possible choices. To rely on simple majority would make all moral issues black and white, and reasonable people would agree that this isn't the case. In most moral gray

---

1   There are three umpires preparing for a baseball game. The youngest umpire says, "Gentlemen, some are balls, some are strikes, but I call them as I see them." An older, wiser umpire responds, "Some are balls, some are strikes, but I call them as they are." The crew chief then says, "Gentlemen, some are balls, some are strikes, but they're nothing until I call them."

areas, from philosophical debates (e.g., the trolley problem[2]) to hot-button issues (e.g., capital punishment), most people are reasonable enough to at least respect the other side, even if they don't agree with it. People also agree that there are clear-cut areas of morality where the dissenting view should not be respected, such as stealing and murder.

However, even in these seemingly clear cases, there will always be a few who don't feel that any given behavior is wrong, no matter how clear the issue may seem to the majority. How many dissenters must exist before the morality of something goes from black and white to gray? It's easy enough to resolve this issue by deciding that everything is a gray area, but there are gradations of gray. For example, the vast, vast majority would agree with the simple statement "stealing is wrong." This would be a fairly black-and-white issue, with only the slightest hints of gray. Something like the trolley problem, however, would be much more evenly split, making it very gray.

Now that we've discussed what is clearly right and wrong and what is a gray area, we must determine how the individual is to respond to gray areas. Do we defer to majority rule? This is impractical, since we don't have the information to know in every situation what the majority would say is right or wrong. Many people choose to seek counsel, either from friends or a moral adviser such as a priest, when faced with a moral quandary. Though this is a highly advisable course of action, as one should always seek more dispassionate, objective perspectives, it is not always an available option

---

2   The trolley problem is a hypothetical ethical dilemma used in philosophical discourse: There is a train on track to kill five people. You can redirect the train to a track where it will kill one person or do nothing and allow the five people to die through inaction. What do you do?

when the decision must be made. Furthermore, there is no guarantee that your adviser will have a better grasp on right or wrong than you. In some professions, ethical boards exist to make and enforce these determinations and, for their part, tend to work fairly well. However, most individuals and moral decisions fall outside their purview, so where does that leave us?

Our individualistic and somewhat libertarian society would argue that, in an area of moral uncertainty, each individual is left to their own devices to decide for themselves what they think is right and what they think is wrong. I take no quarrel with allowing individuals to make their own choices, as people are always free to choose to do wrong. However, I think individuals making their own decisions about what is morally correct is about the stupidest, least accurate way to go about navigating gray areas, as people simply cannot be objective when their own interests and desires are involved. To understand why, it is important to understand why humans have developed their superior intellectual capacity.

Though humans seem to have a moral instinct, what has allowed us to move to the top of the food chain is our intellect. It is often assumed that our intellect's purpose is to help us make more objective, accurate decisions, but this is not the case. At the end of the day, human beings are nothing more than animals, driven by our animalistic drives, desires, and our own self-interest. Our intellect is simply a means to achieve these ends. To reconcile our selfish behavior with our psychological need to view ourselves as moral creatures, our intellect will often deceive us into thinking that whatever our animal instincts drive us to do is morally correct. Thus, if left to their own devices, individuals will not make the morally correct decision. They will do whatever they desire, and their brains will find a way to justify it in moral terms, often by needlessly complicating the issue. A great example of this tension at play is Valjean's soliloquy in *Les Misérables* as he is debating whether to come forward to clear a wrongly accused man.[3]

If individuals cannot be trusted to know what is moral in the face of a gray area, who is to make this decision? This is where I make the argument that organized religion serves a useful social function. Religion can serve to determine right and wrong in ways that individuals cannot by providing a moral code that is detached from the self-interest and hedonistic desires of the individual. It does so through the utilization of collective wisdom and detached objectivity.

Before I go into how religion can serve as the ultimate guidance on right and wrong, let me address the most obvious anticipated objection: that religion is often corrupted by its own self-interest. Well, of course it is. Religion is made up of people, and people are corrupt. People twist and manipulate everything they can to serve their interests and desires. Why should religion be any different? I'm not arguing that religion is a panacea for all of man's imperfections or trying to suggest that its interactions with society and human nature are anything but complicated. I'm simply arguing that it is a tool that can be used for the better or abused for the worse.

I'll pass over any objections about the validity of any particular religious belief by reiterating that theology is not the

---

3   At one point in the musical, Jean Valjean must decide whether to turn himself in or allow an innocent man who's been mistaken for him to go to prison in his place. In his soliloquy, he comes up with all sorts of reasons for allowing an innocent man to go to prison in his place (Valjean employs hundreds of workers, he's turned his life around, he's the mayor of his town, etc.). Though Valjean does the right thing and exonerates the man at his own expense, it's easy to see how a morally weaker individual would use these excuses to justify allowing an innocent to "go to judgment in his place."

topic of this discussion. I'm not denying the truth of any creed or suggesting that religion is nothing more than a tool or social phenomenon. Maybe it is, and maybe it isn't. I don't know, and for our purposes, I don't really care. What's undeniable is that religion has a very real impact on people's behavior—the main topic at hand—and that impact is what I'm interested in.

Since it is hubristic for any individual to assume that they and only they have insight into what is right or wrong, we should rely on collective wisdom. Though no one individual has all the answers, some seem to have greater insight or more unshakable integrity than others. Throughout history, some individuals have been seen as wise men, teachers, prophets, and so on. Society has collected the teachings of these individuals in the form of scripture or other religious texts. These writings have remained relevant for centuries because the useful teachings have remained while the useless or counterproductive ones have fallen off, making these texts great sources of moral wisdom. In the same way, societies have evolved various traditions of morality, because these traditions have proven effective over time. Thus, far from rejecting scripture or traditional morality, we should embrace it as the cream of the moral crop that has survived from generations of experience and social evolution.

Unfortunately, even when someone depends on the wisdom of past generations and great teachers, they run into the same problem individuals generally run into when trying to figure out right and wrong. Particularly, these teachings have to be interpreted, put into context, and applied either generally to today's society or specifically to the moral conflict facing the individual. Individuals making these interpretations themselves will be inclined to twist these teachings in ways that suit their needs and interests. This is where a priestly class of wise individuals comes into play.

By allowing certain individuals to devote their lives to the study and debate of scripture, tradition, and morality, we can rely on them to provide guidance on the morally correct way the rest of us should live our lives. By relying on a class of people instead of a single individual, any biases or errors one person may make will be smoothed out. Of course, even wise individuals can be driven by their own interests and desires, and everyone is liable to be corrupted by the pursuit of wealth and power. It is for this reason that this priestly class must be kept from secular power and detached from earthly concerns, providing only moral guidance to society. This is not to say that there must be a vow of poverty, only that a separation must exist between this class and earthly interests to protect the integrity and objectivity of those handing out moral guidance. In return, society owes a degree of deference to this priestly class where issues of morality are concerned. The detachment of this class, along with their dedication to moral learning, grants them the expertise and objectivity to be best positioned to make moral judgments.

One last note to conclude our discussion of morality. In the above discussion, we often referred to morality in terms of "right" and "wrong," as if they were the only two choices, and in some ways, they are. There is a tendency in Western thought to view things in these absolute terms, as evidenced by the Ten Commandments, many of which start with "thou shalt not..." I would argue that this is not entirely correct and that, rather than being a binary choice, right and wrong are two ends on the moral spectrum. Eastern thought tends to phrase things more in terms of "it is better to..." or "avoid..." and I think this more accurately captures the essence of morality, relative or not. It also acknowledges that while human beings strive to do good and avoid evil, we will not always adhere perfectly to our own moral codes.

I don't think this is a particularly controversial idea. Even the Catholic Church, one of the stalwarts of Western moral thought, acknowledges these distinctions of degree, differentiating between venial and mortal sins. It's difficult to imagine, for example, anybody arguing that telling a lie, though wrong, is comparable to cold-blooded murder. And I don't think anybody would consider sitting at home on the weekend to be wrong, per se, though most would agree it is more right, and thus morally preferable, to volunteer at a soup kitchen. The point is most people intuitively understand and accept this notion, but in discussions of right and wrong, our human instinct to put things into categories and label them leads us to forget this. In allowing morality to guide us, I think this is an important concept to keep in mind.

Granted, there are some facets in which I prefer the Western school of thought. Acknowledging that morality is a spectrum and that nobody will be perfect all the time gives people a cop-out to ignore morality when it's convenient for them. It becomes too easy to dismiss wrongdoing or fail to do something that is right under the guise that you aren't trying to be perfect, or to justify wrongdoing by comparing your trivial sin to a much worse one. It is important to keep in mind that, though perfection can never be achieved, we should strive to do the right thing all the time, no matter how trivial the matter at hand.

THE INTERACTION BETWEEN LAW AND MORALITY

Law and morality are both ways in which society can influence the behavior of individuals in beneficial ways, but they operate very differently and, as such, must be approached differently if they are to have their optimal impact. Traditionally, there has been significant overlap between law and morality, with the moral senses of society often being encoded into law, and moral lapses being punished with force. If something offends people's moral sense, they tend to think there ought to be a law against it. I would argue that this is a mistake. Morality should be idealistic, looking toward how people should be, whereas the law should be pragmatic, made with an eye toward how people actually are.

The reason for such an "ivory tower" approach to morality is that morality must teach people how they should behave. It relies on soft power, convincing people to do the right thing not because they will receive any benefit for doing so or suffer any harm for failing to do so, but because they want to. It teaches us how people should behave in an ideal world and the type of behavior for which we should strive. As such, it may include some teachings, such as nonviolence, that are, at times, impractical in the real world. Morality tells us what behavior is best for society, and this will oftentimes conflict with what we want. It sets a goal for us to strive to achieve and provides guidance to take us in the right direction. However, when there is a conflict between our self-interest and morality, it is still up to the individual to choose to do the right thing. People will often choose to do what is in their interest instead of what is right. Morality should not be altered by knowledge of this fact.

Law should be. Law should be made with a dispassionate eye toward how people are, with all their flaws and imperfections, and should be adjusted accordingly. The purpose of the law should be to modify the behavior of people to achieve the goals of the law-makers. To do so, we must have in mind not only what behavior we want, but also how people will respond to any law we enact. It is not the behavior we should be legislating toward but the response. In other words, making laws should be like playing chess: just as you move in chess based on how you think your opponent will respond to your move, we should make laws based on how people will respond to the altered incentives they create.

This is often not the case. People, in general, don't like to think or accept realities that offend their normative senses, and so rather than think out the best way to modify or extinguish the relevant behavior, their natural instinct is to punish (or reward) the behavior directly. Sometimes this works out fine. Not too many people would argue against laws punishing people for murder or stealing, which seem to serve their purposes fairly well. However, sometimes the causes of the unwanted behavior are complex, and simply banning the behavior may be either ineffective or counterproductive. For example, while it is clearly in society's best interests to limit or elim-inate drug abuse, it has become painstakingly obvious that addicts are going to use drugs despite the legal consequences. In these types of cases, where the causes are complex and humans are going to behave in an undesirable manner regardless of legal consequences, it makes more sense to take a measured, studied, and rational approach to create the best outcomes for society, rather than defaulting to heavy-handed, direct, and overly simplistic legislation.

The fundamental problem lies in human psychology. Though they may deceive themselves into thinking so, for most people, the purpose of passing legislation to address a given situation is not to fix or improve said situation. It's to *feel* like they've done something to fix the problem. Direct, often punitive measures and simple legislation fulfill this basic psychological need, allowing people to sleep easily, telling themselves their concerns are no more, and giving them the feeling of accomplishment that comes from having done some good in this world. Even better, they get this without all that pesky hard work and potential cognitive dissonance that would come from actually developing a strategic, effective solution to the problem and following up to ensure that the solution is working the way it was designed. Passing simple legislation gives an immediate sense of fait accompli: a quick, definitive solution instead of the years of ambiguous, slow improvement that generally results in real solutions.

This problem is aggravated by the fact that self-aggrandizing politicians are eager to take advantage of people's need for security. It's no accident that whenever there is a high-profile case, there will inevitably be a law proposed that follows the format of "[Victim's] Law," a law that, nine times out of ten, will be hastily thrown together, poorly thought out, and do little to address any underlying societal problems. They boil complex issues down to simple slogans and soundbites; then, because they can't rile up the populace or a portion of their voters without acting like they have a solution, they propose meaningless laws that at best have no impact, and at worst exacerbate the situation. Sometimes, this can be as ridiculous as proposing to criminalize behavior that is already illegal.

Law should be designed not on emotions, ideology, or idealism, but on reason. Morality calls for what is best for society, and it is up to each individual to comply with this idealistic vision for society. However, the law cannot enforce this view. Any idealistic, utopian society cannot be created by government but must spring forth from the hearts of the populace. Though the law must also be designed with the best interests of society in mind, it must be more realistic in its goals, setting up a series of punishments and incentives to guide people to engage in behavior that is best for society while recognizing the imperfect, animalistic nature of man, as well as the limited reach of the law.

Think of the law as a game of Plinko.[4] The ball is an individual in society, and the pegs are the laws of that society. The laws can guide and impact what an individual does, but ultimately the ball is going to go where it wants to go. If designed strategically, the pegs can be quite effective in guiding the ball where the designer wants to take it, though ultimately, it is still the ball heading there. In the same way, if designed strategically, the law can alter the incentives of individual behavior in ways that lead people to choose to behave in ways that are beneficial to society, but it cannot force them to do so. Unfortunately, because laws are often written with political, idealistic, or ideological designs, they are often ineffective, sometimes even pushing behavior the opposite way. If our laws are to achieve their goals, they must be written with a detached sense of realism, based on empirical evidence and a logical system of incentives rather than wishful thinking.

HUMAN BEHAVIOR WITHIN SOCIETY

As discussed previously, the defining trait of the so-called "state of nature" is the ability of any individual to act however they please. This trait still defines our lives, even in the world's most

---

4   In Plinko, players drop a ball into the top of a vertical game board. At the bottom of the board are a number of bins marked with different prizes; the player wins the prize of whichever bin the ball lands in. However, between the top of the board and the bins are a number of pegs which will change the course of the ball, requiring some calculations or predictions as to where the ball will actually land.

developed, civilized places. Every day we witness acts of aggression and conduct that would make any of our ancestors feel right at home. The difference is now we label this behavior as crime and give a portion of our income so that other individuals may dedicate their lives to preventing it. However complex a society may be, it all boils down to a series of transactions in which each individual has always had the freedom to engage.

However, it cannot be denied that the society in which we live impacts our behavior. The degree to which this is true is debatable, as even in our most primitive states we lived in protosocieties of clans and tribes consisting of extended families rather than as individuals, but this is ultimately irrelevant. The fundamental difference is that, due to the explicit nature of the law, we no longer have to guess how others expect us to behave or how they will respond to certain behaviors. Our lives today are much more predictable, and, in general, we are much more secure as our ability to defend and provide for ourselves is no longer dependent on our individual strength.

We are animals whose fundamental purpose is to ensure the survival of our genetic material in a much more primitive world, and this is how we are wired. We are not programmed to make fair, accurate, or just decisions, and we aren't programmed to be happy. The strategies and programming that led to our survival in a primitive environment may be counterproductive to our flourishing in an advanced society. The details of this argument are the topic for another book, and too extensive to explore here. The important thing to remember when predicting and evaluating human behavior is this: We aren't programmed for the world in which we live.

CHAPTER 3

The Nature of Politics

This section will focus on the nature of politics and, by extension, history, since history is simply the recorded knowledge of past politics. It will largely describe politics as a function of the interaction, competition, and conflict of various groups. Throughout this section, the objection may arise that political conflicts are sometimes not caused by friction between groups, but through legitimate disagreements within the same group of facts, values, or strategies. Though I would term these political disagreements rather than political conflicts, I do not deny their existence. I would therefore like to start by making a couple of points on this matter.

I do believe that most, if not all, politics can be simplified and discussed in terms of group conflict and interaction, and therefore the model I will lay forth holds true. Nevertheless, there are many issues (abortion, gun control, etc.) that, even though they can be simplified and discussed in terms of conflicting groups, make more sense to discuss in terms of conflicting values, strategies, or (interpretation and knowledge of) facts. Frankly, in my experience, when discussing the politics of the United States, framing the debate in terms of competing values seems to be the most common. This brings me to the main thing that must be kept in mind for this discussion: never get too wrapped up in the box in which an issue is framed.

Framing politics in terms of competing groups or competing values is simply constructing a model by which to make sense of the world. The world—politics in this case—is far too complex and contains way too many variables for our feeble human brains to comprehend. Therefore, we reduce the number of variables or focus on a single facet of human behavior in order to allow ourselves to make sense of an extremely complex system. These models can be incredibly simple or extremely complicated. Often, they start simple and become increasingly complex, and thus, increasingly inaccessible to human thought, as more and more variables are included. They are incredibly useful tools for thinking and understanding the world, but they are not perfect. In the same way that "supply and demand" can help someone understand economics despite being overly simplified, I hope the following section can help make sense of political conflicts in our world.

All politics is tribal in nature. It is the competition of one group of people against another. As social animals, one of our most basic instincts is to affiliate with one another and to form identities around these affiliations. These identities form a critical portion of most people's egos, or views of themselves, and are an integral part of how people see themselves in the context of the world at large. People show a strong preference for fellow group members, or in-group members, over outsiders, or out-group members. There is a natural, instinctive tendency to fight for the survival and prosperity of groups to which you, as an individual, belong. This includes, at times and to varying degrees, prioritizing the well-being of in-group members over that of out-group members, up to and including directly or indirectly causing the death of those out-group members.

The most basic of these is genetic affiliation based on familial ties that can be observed in the clan structure of most prehistorical societies. As humans centralized and human groupings became larger and larger, the idea of who belonged to this fundamental in-group became larger and larger, including larger and larger towns, cities, and ethnic groups, and eventually, entire nations formed around a common cultural or racial identity. Of course, there are other bases for group formation, such as ideology or religion, which will coexist alongside national or ethnic identities, such as Polish Catholic or Lithuanian communist. Sometimes these competing identities coexist peacefully; other times, individuals find themselves torn between their own competing identities. Which identity is most salient depends on the individual, their priorities, and the situation facing them.

People's loyalties tend to run inside-out; that is to say, they care most about their self-interest, followed by their families, their communities, and so on. At the same time, most people will have multiple group identities, including but not limited to a national identity, ethnic identity, religious identity, and often, an ideological identity. The degree to which each individual is attached to each identity will vary from individual to individual, with some individuals being strongly attached to all their in-groups, others clearly prioritizing one or two over others, and some caring only for themselves with little attachment to any of their in-groups. These identities largely drive political behavior.

Politics can fundamentally be boiled down into the competition of one group against another. In our most primitive stage, we competed for control of the basic resources for survival, such as water, food, and shelter. As societies grew more complex, we began to compete for the resources necessary for our society to flourish, most notably land, but also natural resources and trade routes. These competitions play out in a number of ways, from negotiated agreements to outright war, but they all boil down to one thing: power. Politics is intergroup competition over power.

Power, simply defined, is the ability to impact change in the world. It can be hard or soft. Hard power is the ability to impact change directly, and soft power is the ability to impact change indirectly. Hard power is a relatively simple concept to grasp and measure. It refers primarily to military or economic might, as well as anything that can be used to directly cause the result one seeks. Soft power is primarily persuasive, convincing other groups to use their hard power to cause the change one seeks. By way of demonstration, the Civil Rights Movement in the United States was successful not because of Black people's economic or physical might, but because their movement was seen as just, persuading others to cooperate in many of the changes that the movement sought.

The fact that this all boils down to intergroup competition is often difficult to see because it's obscured by the complexity of the interaction between various groups. As mentioned before, most individuals will have multiple group identities, such as a national identity and a religious identity. However, sometimes people will have multiple identities regarding the same quality. Take, for example, the 2014 referendum on Scottish independence. Someone could consider themselves both Scottish and British and thus be torn on how to vote on such an issue. Whether they voted yes or no would likely come down to which identity they consider more central to their self-identity; that is, whether they think of themselves more as a Brit or a Scot.

The simplicity of intergroup competition is further obscured by other factors. First, it's entirely possible for people within a group to have disagreements on what is best for the group, or to have different visions of the world they want to create for their group. In our above example, it's possible that some people thought of themselves more as a Scot than a Brit, but voted to remain, either because they thought it was a better strategic choice for Scotland or because they preferred a world with Scotland in the UK. This would lead them to vote in the same manner as someone prioritizing their British identity.

Furthermore, there are groups based on other facets of identity, such as religion or ideology, that also come into play. To go back to the Civil Rights Movement, the movement can be boiled down to competition between Black Americans and white Americans. However, there were many white Americans who joined in and supported the Civil Rights Movement. Why? Part of the answer is the effectiveness of the Black Americans' exercise of soft power. Civil rights activists effectively garnered support for their cause through their courage, nonviolence, and the persuasiveness of their arguments. However, there is another reason related to identity that led white Americans to support the Civil Rights Movement: in addition to thinking of themselves as white, they also thought of themselves as Christian, liberal, or simply as a just person, and were motivated by these facets of their identity to act.

THE PURSUIT OF SELF-INTEREST

Many analyses and explanations of human behavior, particularly in the field of economics, start with the assumption that human beings act with rational self-interest. As flawed as this idea is, it provides a decent starting point to examine human political behavior, with a few noted caveats and modifications.

The first is to dispel the myth that human beings are rational. The thought seems to be that, because humans are the most intelligent animals, we are primarily intelligent animals. We are not. Human intellectual capacity, though superior to that of any other animal on the planet, is still riddled with biases, heuristics, and fallacies. Some of these may have served us well in evolutionary times. Some may serve us well today. However, the fact remains that human beings act far more emotionally than they do rationally. Though people tend to think they are acting rationally, generally they are acting out of some aspect of their instinctive, irrational brain without realizing it. This interferes with the rationality of their actions.

Furthermore, even when people are capable of putting their emotions aside to pursue their self-interest, the strategy they choose will often be imperfect. People are intelligent animals, but they are not perfectly intelligent. They make mistakes, even when they are trying to do the rational thing. This is compounded by the fact that the same biases mentioned before creep into human strategic thinking. People often fail to pursue rational self-interest simply because they are unsure how to best go about it.

There is also ambiguity concerning what, rationally, is in one's self-interest. What are the ends one is trying to pursue? If I have some free time, should I go to the gym, read a book, or take a nap? There is no rational right or wrong answer to this question. It comes down to a matter of preference. Therefore, adding "rational" to our discussion of self-interest seems only to add unnecessary complexity and confusion. Instead of pursuing their rational self-interest or rationally pursuing their self-interest, let us simply say that people will generally pursue their self-interest.

This requires us to more neatly explore what is meant by self-interest. At first glance, self-interest seems obvious, as does the fact that people don't always act in their self-interest. I would argue that, aside from simple mistakes, humans do always act in their self-interest. However, the interest may be more than simply a material interest, and the self may refer to something more than the individuals themselves. In other words, acting for the good of others can, at times, be a form of self-interest.

Even when looking out for themselves, people are not always motivated by simple, material interests. By conventional standards, a person who gives money to charity would not be said to be acting out of self-interest. However, when you consider that, in addition to their material needs, people have ego needs—in this case, the need to see themselves as a charitable person—that is exactly what they are doing. Giving money away feeds into their self-image, which may be more important to them than the money itself. Remember, Maslow's hierarchy of needs contains a whole host of needs that must be satisfied. Which ones are motivating the behavior depends on the individual and the situation, but at the end of the day, it is still the individual acting in self-interest by fulfilling their own needs.

Maslow's Hierarchy of Needs

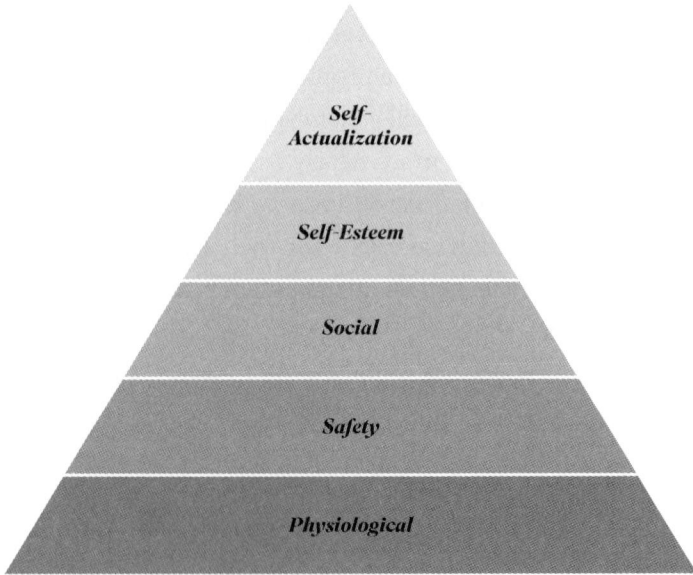

Acting "selflessly" can also be in an individual's self-interest where these higher needs are not relevant. We are not designed by evolution to survive; we are designed by evolution to pass on our genetic material. Therefore, self-interest is not necessarily what promotes our own survival and prosperity but that of our genetics. This is why a mother will give her life to defend her child, or soldiers will risk their lives in defense of their country. We are programmed to care about group survival, and sometimes ensuring the survival of our genetics means putting others in front of ourselves. We can call this extended self-interest, essentially self-interest by proxy, with simple self-interest being the tendency to look out for yourself more directly.

This is easy to see when it comes to parents sacrificing for their children, but why would people put their lives on the line to help strangers? The soldier who defends his nation doesn't know the vast majority of people for whom he or she fights. One answer is that nations do tend to be organized through some biological commonality, so even if you are not sacrificing for your direct relatives, there is a genetic incentive to look out for group welfare. However, this incentive is insufficient to explain the behavior, as we see the same type of self-sacrifice for the common good even in groups where there is no biological link, such as religious or ideological groups. How can sacrificing for these groups be in an individual's self-interest? Aside from the aforementioned concerns of self-image, this can be explained both through extended and simple self-interest.

The extended self-interest concern is more central to our discussion, and powerful enough that people will, in some circumstances, sacrifice their lives to satisfy it. The short answer is that the same instinctive, psychological drives that lead us to defend our kin get applied to any group to which we belong. Whether this is evolutionarily beneficial or simply a generalization of the specific evolutionary drive to ensure our genetic survival is a debate for another day, but the point is that people, on some level aware of their own mortality,[5] are highly motivated to ensure the survival and prosperity of their in-groups. This motivation is so strong that it can override their instincts to ensure their own prosperity and, at times, their own survival.

There is also a simple self-interest motive that at least warrants a mention. The basis of all virtue is to put the well-being of society above that of oneself, and society tends to reward what it

---

5   For example, Terror Management Theory posits that individuals deal with the fear of their own mortality by more tightly embracing their cultural values.

sees as virtuous behavior. Look at the esteem in which we hold firefighters, police officers, and soldiers. This social status carries with it benefits, and virtuous individuals inspire others to follow in their footsteps. Furthermore, societies consistently despise those who benefit at the expense of the greater good, and this has negative consequences. In essence, virtue creates its own rewards through social reinforcement.

For example, if I were a soldier going into battle, my best choice would not be to lead the charge; it would be to hide in the back under the food cart. However, the negative consequences of being branded a coward (not to mention any legal consequences) are enough to prevent me from doing so. Furthermore, though leading the charge creates a greater immediate risk to my survival, I might decide it's worth it for the positive rewards of being seen as a war hero. By creating concepts of "virtue" and social rewards for "virtuous" behavior, society encourages individuals to act in ways that are good for society at the expense of their immediate self-interest.

As with most things, there are huge individual differences in how people prioritize their self-interest against the interests of the group. Though there are extreme cases, with some individuals showing no concern for group welfare and others being much more self-sacrificing, most people fall somewhere in between, trying to balance the interests of the group with their own interests. Though the reasons for these differences are interesting, they are neither concerning nor surprising, as humans exhibit strong individual differences in most things. The important point is that looking out for the well-being of the group is a form of self-interest, and this extended self-interest is what motivates most, if not all, political behavior.

Politics, then, is simply the pursuit of (mostly extended) self-interest. If there is such a simple explanation for political behavior, why are politics so complicated? It's for much the same reason the economy is so complicated even though it's just the aggregate of simple transactions. There are a lot of people belonging to a lot of groups pursuing a lot of contradictory and complementary interests, leading to the often-referenced strange bedfellows. Even individual behavior can be complex, as individuals belong to a number of groups with a revolving door of relevancy in regard to motivating their behavior.

To demonstrate this more concretely, let's take a look at one of the simplest groups we belong to: being an American or any other national identity. There seems to be this prevalent idea, especially among moderates and the relatively apolitical, that, despite our political differences, we are all Americans and just want what's best for our country. We all have the same ends—good schools, safe streets, and a prosperous economy. We just disagree on which means best achieve our intended ends. While there is some truth to this view, it misses the main point. Debate over the most effective means to shared ends makes up a relatively small portion of political disagreement; most of it is caused by different groups with different ends.

Looking at foreign policy, it is traditionally the case that we all want basically the same thing. This is because, in this arena, we are all Americans looking to protect American ideals and interests. It is for this reason that politics has been said to end at the borders. Though there is some intergroup conflict domestically, particularly from pacifists or human rights activists who prioritize their ideological groups over their national group, most of the conflict on foreign policy is over what is best for America.

The relevant group being American, we are all on the same team.

With regard to domestic politics, this is not the case. Though it may seem that way when you put the goals in broad terms such as a good economy or public safety, the question quickly becomes a good economy for whom? Policies that benefit the economy on the whole may disproportionally favor certain groups, such as the wealthy. Trade policies may benefit the overall economy but will harm certain industries while helping others. Public safety can cause tension between law enforcement groups and those they police. Broadly stating the goals of public policy masks the complexity of these issues.

The fact is that in any society there are countless groups to consider, and this gives way to its complexity. There are law enforcement groups, the military, journalists, economic classes, racial groups, and industry groups, and this is simply scratching the surface. Furthermore, though some of these groups are limited to one region or one country, others are transnational. Every individual will belong to multiple groups, prioritize their memberships in each group differently, and act according to their group interests. To further complicate things, these groups overlap. For example, it's common to see people support law enforcement not because they are law enforcement themselves, but because they have relatives in law enforcement.

This is complicated even further by the fact that groups don't have clear-cut, static interests. Some groups have complementary interests, and others have contradictory interests. Some groups with generally contradictory interests may agree on a single or a handful of issues, or the inverse can occur. Any given individual will belong to a number of groups and have to decide how to balance the various interests. For any given individual, the group relevant to motivating their political views and actions is likely to change depending on what the issue is. Two individuals may act as members of the same union on one issue and then disagree on another due to conflicting religious beliefs. These shifting sets of group interests and alliances produce the amazing complexity that is politics.

It is for this reason that political conflicts often can't be resolved by simply coming together and talking it out in a well-reasoned manner. Such an approach can and often does work when the parties involved in the conflict have the same interests. We should set policies to achieve our goals based on empirical evidence and rationality. However, this approach can only take us so far. At some point, we will have to decide which group interest to prioritize. When the choice is between security and individual rights, or economic growth and environmental protections, there is no objective right or wrong answer that can be achieved through rational, reasoned debate. There is innate, intergroup conflict that makes up the core of politics.

How we resolve these conflicts varies greatly across time and space, along with the relationships between the groups in conflict. Historically, probably the most common resolution has been violence, with the most extreme form of violence resulting in genocide. In most of the Western world today, the preferred method is democracy. We simply vote and accept to resolve the issue in accordance with whatever method has been set out in the laws of the land. This is more effective, so long as the losing side accepts their loss. In the next section, we will take a brief look at the history of the Anglo-American people, the methods we've evolved to resolve conflict, and the role these methods have played in the ascendency of Great Britain, followed by the United States.

PART II

Historical and Political Analysis

In this part, we will take the philosophical building blocks we just discussed and apply them in a real-world context. We will start with history, examining an abbreviated history of the Anglo-American people and the rise of both Great Britain and the United States to global predominance. Two explanations will be offered for this success—situational and ideological.

We will also look at individual rights and how the fair application of these rights has helped these societies prosper. We will then take the lessons we've learned from history and see how we can apply them to create a stronger approach to politics, governance, and policymaking. Finally, we will look at a very general agenda we should pursue for our nation and how to best resolve conflicts among ourselves.

CHAPTER 4

The History of the Anglo-American People

The last half-millennium of human history has been dominated by the Anglo-American people. The first iteration of this was the British Empire, an empire so expansive it spanned the globe. In the first half of the twentieth century, British power gave way to American hegemony as the former British colony fully realized its potential. During this time, Anglo-American legal and democratic norms have largely become global norms, and English has become the language of international business and relations. What was it that led to Anglo-American preeminence? Is it coincidental that the last two hegemonic powers derive from a shared culture, or is there something about Anglo-American society that preordains prosperity?

Not surprisingly, the history of the Anglo-American people starts on the island of Great Britain. In Roman times, this island was populated by a Celtic people known as the Britons. After the fall of the Roman Empire, from about AD 500-1000, a number of Germanic tribes began to immigrate onto the island, pushing the native Celtic people west into Wales and north into Scotland. These German people formed the seven Anglo-Saxon kingdoms, which eventually united all of England, though not Scotland or Wales. The Norman Conquest in 1066 put William the Conqueror on the English throne and marked (for our purposes) the beginning of Anglo-American history.

The next 500 years of Anglo-American history are marked by turmoil and war, as is pretty much all of European history at this time. The Kingdom of England fought a series of wars in France over the claims of their royals, conquered Wales, and fought amongst themselves in the War of the Roses. Most importantly, in 1215 the Magna Carta was agreed to by King John, and though its actual implementation was less than smooth, it established the idea that there were certain rights that could not be infringed by the government. This concept of individual rights, along with the English common law that began to evolve around this time, make up the core of Anglo-American legal life.

The next major mile marker in our extremely brief and simplified journey through Anglo-American history is the defeat of the Spanish Armada in 1588. This naval victory established the Royal Navy as the premier naval force in the world. At a time when colonialism was taking off, the importance of this is difficult to overstate. First off, with Great Britain being an island, having naval supremacy made them near immune to invasion, allowing them to focus on expansion without having to worry about their own territory being invaded. Furthermore, naval supremacy allowed the British to control trade routes, helping secure the economic prosperity that would mark the keystone of the British Empire.

Finally, we can't speak of Anglo-American history without speaking about America. The colonization of America took the culture, laws, and ideas that had been developed in England and transported them onto a new continent. The independence of the

United States in 1776 marked an opportunity for Anglo-American culture to prosper free of external threats and on a continent rich in resources. Though British power would eventually fade, it would be replaced by a child nation, one that shared its language, values, and laws, and has, at least since the turn of the twentieth century, been its closest ally. Whether it was merely a historical happenstance that a nation with a shared culture and heritage succeeded Britain as the premier global power or whether there is something unique about that culture that caused it will be explored in the next section.

THE SITUATIONAL EXPLANATION FOR ANGLO-AMERICAN SUCCESS

The first explanation for why Anglo-American culture rose to dominate the world for the last 500 years is probably the simplest of the two. It presupposes that there is nothing unique or special about Anglo-American culture, and it is just a coincidence that Britain was followed at the top of the food chain by another superpower with the same culture, values, and legal system. This isn't a particularly ridiculous idea. Let's pass over the reasons Europe,[6] rather than the Americas, Africa, or Asia, became the most powerful region of human civilization. Once Europe became supreme, human nature made it inevitable that Europe would dominate the globe.

There are reasons beyond luck of the draw to think that

---

6   While I'm passing over the reasons in this work, I think the reasons are laid out well in *Guns, Germs, and Steel* by Jared Diamond. Additionally, below I pass over the reasons why Europe's colonization of the Americas was successful, but I think the book *1491* by Charles Mann covers the topic thoroughly.

Britain, rather than, say, France or Spain, would rise to European supremacy. Most notable among these is the fact that Great Britain is an island. Throughout history, Europe has been the armpit of wars, with each country stuck in a constant cycle of invasion and counterinvasion. Great Britain, on the other hand, has not been invaded since the Normans pulled off the feat in 1066. This sheltered the British from the constant destruction invading armies wreaked on the rest of the continent. Perhaps more importantly, it led to the development of the most important weapon in Britain's arsenal: the Royal Navy.

Being an island nation, it would make sense that the focus of Britain's military development would be its naval force. All Britain needed was to prevent anyone from crossing the British Channel, and it would be immune to invasion, safe in its own little fortress to act in the world at will. Had history remained predominantly regional, this might have been the extent of British success. It could have remained stuck, safe on its island but lacking the resources to expand. However, its naval supremacy positioned Britain perfectly to operate when politics moved from the regional to the global arena.

It's no accident that Britain's ascendancy as the global power coincides with the colonial era. Britain itself is a relatively small island with limited resources and potential. The colonial period allowed it to use its naval power to utilize resources across the globe. By controlling the oceans, it could control trade routes and the movement of armies and resources on the waters. This allowed it to expand its capacity far beyond that of its home island, all the while protecting its base of operations from direct attack.

Taking this view of things, America would inevitably become Britain on steroids. Once Europeans discovered the Americas, human nature made it inevitable that they would attempt to settle it and take it over, and, for a myriad of reasons,[7] they succeeded. For the reasons discussed above, once this happened, it was likely, if not unavoidable, that Britain would be the most successful in doing so, leading to a predominantly British culture in North America. Even though this explanation of history assumes there was nothing special about British culture, any new nation in North America was destined for greatness once thrown into the new, Europe-led global political arena.

First, and most obviously, the United States had the same basic advantage as Britain. It was, in essence, an island nation. Obviously, the United States wasn't literally an island like Britain. However, it had no powerful enemies with whom to contend. It was bordered by two oceans and colonial powers on either side. As such, aside from a few minor, nonexistential scraps with the British, the United States was able to grow at its own pace, unthreatened by a rival power and unharmed by war. Throughout its history, the United States has more or less been able to engage other nations on its own terms, allowing it to enter the fray only in situations where it would benefit the United States.

Though the United States didn't develop the naval supremacy and colonial proclivity that marked Britain's ascendancy, it never needed to. Geographically, the United States is huge. It has such natural geographic diversity and is so rich in natural resources that it was able to support itself without expansion beyond the borders of the continent itself. The United States expanded, faced with opposition only from the weakened native populations and able to access whatever resources it needed much more easily

---

7   See Mann's *1491* referenced in the previous footnote.

than European powers. Just as importantly, today the population of the United States is just under half the combined population of Europe. This wealth of population and resources, combined with the relative security of its location, makes it not at all surprising that the United States would rise as a global power.

This truncated version of history is an intentionally insufficient explanation of why the Anglo-American nations have, in turn, risen to the top of the global food chain. The purpose is not to give a detailed history or draw out a thesis as to the exact reasons why history has played out the way it has. It would be impossible to know if such a history is an accurate account of events, or simply an attempt to retroactively explain why things played out the way they did. Nor is the purpose of the section to make an argument that the United States and Great Britain rose to supremacy by mere serendipity or exclusively for the above-stated situational reasons. It is simply to provide a contrast with the next section, in which I argue that ideological and cultural reasons have led to our ascendancy, and to point out that an alternative, logically valid explanation of history does exist.

THE IDEOLOGICAL EXPLANATION FOR ANGLO-AMERICAN SUCCESS

The other explanation is that there is something innate about Anglo-American civilization that sets it up for success. This is similar to the idea of American Exceptionalism, expanded to the entire Anglo-American world, though hopefully with fewer moralistic undertones. The basic idea is that Anglo-American culture is what led to the success of Great Britain and the United States, rather than the situational causes mentioned above. In other words, the Anglo-American people would have seen the same rise whether they had originated in England or anywhere else in the world.

First, a side note. These two explanations of Anglo-American success are not mutually exclusive, nor are they necessarily competing. In fact, I would argue that they are complementary. It's entirely possible that Anglo-American culture would have led to success wherever it emerged, and that any people, given the situational advantages discussed above, would have thrived. It's also possible that, though Anglo-American culture is directly responsible for the success of the Anglo-American people, this culture could not have emerged without the security Britain's island geography afforded them. Any other possible combination or interaction between the two explanations is possible as well. They are discussed separately for convenience, not because one must be chosen over the other.

So, what are the ideological factors that made the Anglo-American people great? The first is tradition and continuity. Unlike other people, the English and American people have not had complete breakdowns of their social and political systems. There have been attempts to create completely new socio-political orders, to be sure, but none have succeeded, aside from Oliver Cromwell's short-lived success in the mid-1600s. Changes to the English and American political systems have occurred, but they've been slow and incremental, allowing stability over time. This is in stark contrast to other nations, such as France, Russia, and Germany, that have seen traumatic, quick changes to the social order.

In Britain, you've seen more or less the same form of governance since 1066. It's no accident that the Magna Carta, dating from 1215, is still considered a crucial document in the history of the present-day Anglo-American legal system. There have been tensions, wars, and changes, but never successful, full-scale destruction of the existing system. Part of the reason for this has been the unique flexibility of the British monarchy. They have accepted, over time, more and more limitations on their power, to the point that the monarch in the present day is little more than a figurehead. The flexibility of the system allowed the British political system to adapt and change with the times, slowly incorporating more modern and democratic ideals without facing the chaos and upheaval that accompanied such changes in other nations.

The same basic pattern can be seen in the much younger American government. The United States has, since 1789, operated under the exact same Constitution, yet the American government of today would be unrecognizable to the Founding Fathers. This is entirely by design. The drafters of the Constitution recognized that the governing needs of their day may be entirely different from those of future generations, so they built in a process (the amendment process) to allow future generations to alter the document. Even where directly amending the Constitution is not involved, the government of the United States has been able to evolve with time, most notably in the power of the President and the Executive Branch. Again, this has allowed the United States to keep up with the ever-changing needs of the world without the destruction and regression that comes with sudden, violent revolutions.

This respect for tradition, coupled with the flexibility to incorporate change over time, has allowed both the British and the Americans to experience stability that has enhanced their ability to grow and operate on the world stage. Allowing the expression and redress of grievances within the existing political system prevents domestic grievances and dissatisfaction from boiling over into the full-fledged revolutions that have plagued other societies. Keeping domestic strife to a minimum has allowed for greater mobilization of the population in times of war, allowed the focus to remain on shared goals rather than differences, and given leaders the freedom to focus on defending the nation as a whole rather than fighting domestic foes. This isn't to say there aren't divisions or domestic rivalries within both Great Britain and the United States. It simply means that resolving these disagreements through ballots instead of battles (with a few notable exceptions) has allowed a degree of stability and continuity that has allowed the Anglo-American people to prosper.

It could be argued that this is more a situational explanation than an ideological one. Perhaps the continuity of Anglo-American governments has been nothing more than a winning streak, or perhaps the continuity is the result of the success afforded by the situational factors presented above. In other words, perhaps the Anglo-American people have stability because they are strong, rather than being strong because they have stability. This merely serves to accentuate the point that the situational and ideological factors play into each other, rather than being two distinct explanations. It is likely that neither circumstance nor ideology is sufficient to fully explain Anglo-American success, although which you give more weight to may inform the future path for both nations.

Nevertheless, this "chicken or the egg" debate is worth a side trip because it illuminates a more general point. Part of the reason for this stability is that the Anglo-American people have tended to reject rigid, extremist ideologies in favor of pragmatism. This may be either cultural or situational, as we have seen that extremist ideologies tend to prosper when times are toughest, as illustrated by the rise of Nazism in interwar Germany or Communism preceding the Bolshevik Revolution. Whether Britain and the United States have avoided extremism because times have never gotten as tough, or times have never gotten as bad because they've avoided extremism is a difficult determination to make. The point is that we must be proactive in anticipating and compromising to deal with potential problems before they become too large. The longer a problem is allowed to persist, the larger it becomes, and the more people embrace extremist ideologies, which in turn makes the problem even harder to address. We see this today in American politics. As America's situation worsens, the parties become more extreme, making compromise more difficult, which leads to the situation deteriorating further, driving extremism further and making compromise still more difficult. It's a self-perpetuating cycle that, if not stopped, will end in destruction.

Returning to the ideological factors that drove Anglo-American success, we must now consider the most important: the rule of law. The Anglo-American legal system that developed over the last thousand years has done more than simply deliver the most just mechanism for dealing with crime and punishment and righting civil wrongs. It has provided a set of rules by which society can govern itself. By establishing a set of rules, respecting them, and applying them consistently, Anglo-American society has afforded itself one of the most efficient forms of government in the history of the world. This is directly responsible for its success.

The efficiency of the system Anglo-Americans have developed for resolving disputes comes from it being accessible and legitimate—it does not rely on self-help. By accessible, I mean that it is open to all members of society, and by legitimate, I mean that it is widely respected enough that the outcomes it produces are consistently accepted. These two features allow individuals to rely on the system put in place by society rather than self-help, allowing society to avoid the violence and inefficiencies that occur when people choose or are forced to take matters into their own hands. The fact that self-help is generally punished helps to deter the problem.

Part of the legitimacy of the Anglo-American justice system derives from the fact that legal principles are applied consistently. In the early days, you had individual judges deciding cases and writing decisions based on the proper outcome. However, since individuals can disagree on the proper outcome in close cases, as the law evolved, there has been an effort on the part of judges to follow past rulings. This development of precedents and common law allows for consistent decisions that provide the predictability and stability needed for society to prosper.

This consistency and stability carry over to the political arena. By providing elections and a clear-cut system to resolve political disputes, political quarrels have been resolved in a way accepted by the entire population, and we have avoided the intra-societal violence that has plagued and, at times, destroyed other nations. Transitions of power are necessary in all societies. The Anglo-American system ensures that these transitions are smooth and effective.

The most important feature of the rule of law is the way in which it protects and ensures individual rights. Whether specifically enumerated in the Constitution or simply respected by the legal system, ensuring that individuals are protected and secure has numerous effects that allow society to prosper. First off, ensuring that all individuals feel protected and respected by society gives everyone a personal stake in society's well-being. It encourages individuals to innovate and take risks, knowing that the rewards and gains they make from their own industry will be protected. It also attracts talent, drawing hardworking and skilled people from societies where they don't feel protected to a society where they will.

If this section seems overly idealistic or naïve, that's probably because it is. Clearly, the Anglo-American justice system has its flaws and does not always work as well in practice as it does in theory. But this same criticism can be made of any society in any place at any time. The Anglo-American system is simply superior to the other flawed, broken systems that history has churned out. We should always be attempting to improve our system, while at the same time recognizing the value of the system and the key role it has played in our society's success.

It also must be pointed out that the Anglo-American system works well precisely because it is a system. There have been countless societies throughout history that have seen great success while under the leadership of a talented individual or group. This success is inevitably short-lived when these individuals pass from this mortal coil to be replaced by less talented leaders or chaos and turmoil. Because it is the system of the Anglo-Americans, designed or evolved, that has led to our success, it is not beholden to the talents of a few. Though we've had talented leaders, our system has allowed our society to keep functioning at a high level even after they've left us.

Since history is nothing more than the sum of every action of every individual, much of the rest of the book will focus on individuals. Even though it is the system that has led to success, this system is still made up of individuals whose actions are influenced by the society in which they live. We will begin by discussing the significance (or lack thereof) of the individual, the rights that society has chosen to afford individuals, and how an individual ought to behave in society.

CHAPTER 5

The Role of the Individual in History

Individuals are both entirely insignificant and the basic building block of all human history. The most relevant unit in discussing history or politics is groups, and the group is the only thing that matters. The individual is to the group as a cell is to the human body. The individual will inevitably die, but the group can live on as long as it has members willing to support it and work for its survival. The purpose of every individual is to promote the health, well-being, and survival of their in-groups. This primary motivation was likely caused by evolution to promote the survival of one's DNA and was originally and most strongly directed toward members of one's own family. This instinctive drive can be generalized, however, to any group to which an individual belongs.

At the same time, all of human society and history is nothing more than individual action—all societies and systems are nothing more than a collection of individual actions. If society constrains or influences an individual's behavior, it is only because that individual is predicting how other individuals will react to their behavior. If any system works, it is only because individuals have accepted and follow a set of rules for how to deal with the actions of and conflicts with other individuals. In the same way that a human body can be broken down into systems, which can be broken down into organs, which can ultimately be broken down into cells, any human society can be broken down into individuals.

So, which is it? Are individuals important or insignificant? Objectively, it's a matter of perspective. In a cosmic or historical sense, a single human life is insignificant, but if you examine a smaller time frame or more local scale, a single human life can be incredibly significant. It has about the same significance as a single atom: unimportant broadly, but critically important in the composition of a molecule. More importantly, however, the value of human life is a subjective, moral argument for priests and philosophers, beyond the scope of this work. Suffice it to say that human life has the value we place upon it, and nothing more.

If human life holds the value we place on it, what rights do individuals possess by nature of being human? The answer, again, is the rights we choose to give them. They are entitled, by nature, to nothing. Humans are nothing more than highly intelligent animals, and nature allows any animal to take any action they so choose, up to and including harming or killing other animals. Nature is replete with examples of animals killing other animals, humans included. Clearly, no law of nature protects the life, liberty, or property of any individual from infringement by another. Thus, the very idea of rights is something derived by society to ensure the protection and prosperity of all who respect the rights of others. Rights are no more than a social construct, turtles stacked upon turtles with no foundation.

The fact that rights are a social construct should not be taken to mean that they are insignificant. Social constructs are very powerful, if for no other reason than people accept them to be true and, thus, they influence the individual behavior that makes up the core of human social life. It also doesn't necessarily mean that they are wrong. Social constructs provide a common basis for understanding that allows us to function with one another more efficiently. To acknowledge that human rights are a social construct is to recognize that rights are what society has agreed to grant each individual and will exist only so long as they are broadly recognized and respected. There is nothing innate about them.

The rights granted to an individual have differed dramatically over time and from culture to culture. More often than not, rights are granted only to the dominant group in society, though in modern Western culture there has been an increasing tendency to grant rights to all. Even today, the exact rights that are granted to a human being are a matter of debate both between and within nations, most notably between the United States and Europe. To give just a few examples, most European countries view healthcare as a right that must be granted to all, while the United States does not. On the flip side, few European countries have the same respect for free speech or gun rights that is widespread in the United States and enshrined in the U.S. Constitution. Neither of these are right or wrong. They are simply different.

Though there is no wrong answer to what rights individuals have, what is important is that they are widely accepted so that other individuals, most importantly the collection of individuals organized into what we call a government, do not infringe on them. It is also important that the rights are enforced; that is, that third parties are willing to intervene when a right is infringed upon, either by an individual or because it is a positive right. A positive right is a right to have someone, usually the government, do something for you, such as a right to be provided healthcare or education. This contrasts with the more common (at least in America) concept of negative rights, the right to not have something done to you, such as having your privacy violated.

If there is no obligation to do so, why have individual rights at all? There is a pretty obvious moral answer here that it's simply the right thing to do, but I'm going to skip over that part because it already seems to be accepted by most in our society. Moral arguments aside, there is a related, preference component. A preference answer means that we like something better than the alternative, without attaching any moral or value judgment to it. I can prefer beef to chicken without necessarily saying or thinking eating beef is better in any way. I simply like it better (objectively, it's worse).

Preference components come up in a democracy and in governing human society. Sometimes, there are questions that don't have an empirically right answer and that can't be answered in a moral sense. It's simply a matter of deciding what type of society we would prefer to live in. Not surprisingly, there is often an overlap with moral arguments, as people have a tendency to associate what they want with what is right, but a preference argument removes that judgment. Moral arguments aside, my guess is that most people prefer to live in a society where their rights are respected and are willing to respect the rights of others in exchange. It simply makes for a more pleasant existence when you are not constantly attacked or bullied, and when you have an agreed-upon range of liberty and action.

There is another argument that has nothing to do with morality or preferences, and that is that respecting individual rights allows for a stronger, more efficient society. How persuasive you find this argument probably depends on whether you found ideological or situational explanations for Anglo-American success more persuasive in the previous section. The basic idea is that, by respecting individual rights, you are maximizing the group's human capital by allowing individuals to grow and prosper, which in turn leads the group to flourish.

This is most clearly seen and recognized in economics. In fact, it is often argued that the Anglo-American world's tendency to embrace laissez-faire economics is one of the reasons for its economic prosperity. By protecting property rights, individuals are willing to devote their own time and resources to economic development, since they know they will be able to benefit from what they create. There would be very different incentives for individuals if they had to worry about somebody taking anything they'd earned, or if they had to devote resources to defending it themselves.

This idea is easy to see in basic economic areas such as farming and industry, but it also applies to research. Patent law allows people to patent the ideas they develop and benefit from them, encouraging economic and scientific innovation. By protecting the rights of people who develop ideas, we are encouraging innovation, allowing people to devote more time and resources to research and development than they could if they had to worry about protecting their ideas, or if they knew they weren't going to be able to recover the resources they'd poured into their research.

This is also the concept behind freedom of speech and the marketplace of ideas. People exist across a spectrum, with a wide degree of ideological variance. The idea is that by allowing for an open and honest debate, we are allowing the concept of the free market to apply to ideas. Everyone can throw out what they think, no matter how insane or extreme those ideas are, and people will naturally gravitate toward the best ideas. By respecting the individual right to political expression, we are allowing society to determine which ideas are most effective, and which ideas to embrace or reject.

In addition to the benefits individual rights provide to the individual, which in turn benefit society by strengthening its component parts, the respect of individual rights provides a direct benefit to society at large, and the government in particular. There are simply things that the government, no matter how powerful, cannot control. Most of these things involve, on one level or another, the expression of individual rights. By taking a more hands-off approach, the government does not waste its time, resources, or energy trying to control things it cannot.

By doing this, the government also decreases corruption and abuses of power and thus increases its legitimacy and the willingness of the people to cooperate and comply without the need for force. When a government attempts to overregulate individual behavior, the mere logistics of enforcing such a large number of laws becomes impossible. Since all law enforcement boils down to the individual decision of one government official to actually enforce a law, laws end up being enforced at the whim of the enforcer. Think of a speeding ticket. Whether or not somebody is given a speeding ticket largely depends on whether the police officer feels like giving them one. Though this is a minor example, the problem becomes more evident when the laws and punishments become more serious. Such inconsistent enforcement and widespread discretion open the door for government officials to abuse their power, or worse, become corrupt.

Overregulation and well-intentioned laws also tend to

produce a lot of unintended consequences. People do not always respond to laws as simply and predictably as we'd like. Sometimes, passing a law to have one effect can produce the opposite. Prohibition may well have increased alcohol consumption. Many sex offenders have responded to strict restrictions on their lives by failing to register and going off the grid. By keeping laws relatively simple, the government avoids having to deal with unintended fallout from unnecessary laws.

As a result, any person or ideology looking to strengthen the group should embrace individual rights and freedoms, since they make the group stronger. This is proven by the success of Anglo-American civilizations; though, the degree to which this is true depends on the relative weight you give to ideological or situational factors. If we, as Americans, want to make our country stronger, we should ride the horse that got us here, accepting and embracing the Constitutional rights of all Americans, simply because they are the rights we have agreed to grant to our fellow citizens. We should respect the Constitution because it lays out the rules we have agreed to play by and the rights that are granted to all. It is not our place to decide which Constitutional rights to respect or to whom they apply. Going down that path leads to the denigration and eventual collapse of a system that has led to an unprecedented level of stability and prosperity.

INDIVIDUAL RIGHTS AND THEIR APPLICATION

It's all well and good to have an ivory tower, philosophical discussion of the rights of individuals and to establish principles and so forth, but all this intellectualism does no good unless these rights are applied in the real world. In this section, we will focus more on how individual rights must be applied in order for them to have any practical application. Any right we choose to grant to an individual should be granted in a consistent manner to all individuals, regardless of whether the views they express are popular or within the societal mainstream. All societies protect the expression of popular views and popular individuals. For our grant of basic rights to have the positive social impact discussed above, they must be applied in the same manner to unpopular individuals and unpopular views.

Again, this is easier said than done. Most Americans will agree with the above statements here when discussed in the abstract, but many quickly change their tune when they find out Nazis want to march in Skokie. The fact is that people very quickly form opinions on the individuals expressing their rights, identifying them as either one of "us" or one of "them," and then decide whether they support the rights of the individuals based on whether or not they happen to like them. People, at times, will even go so far as to explicitly deny an individual their rights because of who they are, outright saying that because they're a Nazi (or whatever unpopular group you choose), they don't deserve rights. This leads to people taking wildly inconsistent positions on how rights such as freedom of expression should be applied based on to whom we are applying those rights.

To demonstrate this inconsistency more concretely, let's take a look at two American controversies of the twenty-first century. Around the 2010 midterm elections, Sarah Palin released a map showing targets over the Congressional districts of Democrats that she was targeting for defeat in the election. After the 2016 election, comedienne Kathy Griffin posed for a photo shoot with the decapitated head of Donald Trump. Both incidents set off a wave of controversy, and both used symbolic messages of violence to make a political point. In a broad sense, both offended people in the same way for the same reasons.

However, the people getting offended by each incident were likely different. Though I have no direct empirical evidence with which to back up this assertion, I imagine a number of people who were defending Kathy Griffin in 2017 were calling for Sarah Palin's (metaphorical) head in 2010, and vice versa. With the similarities in content, why the discrepancy in response? Because one is a Democrat and the other a Republican. Though there are likely some who were upset by both and others who defended both, my guess is that many people were okay with the delivery when they liked the message, but more than willing to take advantage of a potential weapon with which to target a political adversary when the situation reversed.

The point is not to argue that either woman was right or wrong in what she said or how she said it. The point is that, for many people, their offense or lack thereof is based more on factionalism than fairness. Again, the primary motivating political behavior is group allegiance, the drive to defend one's own groups while attacking hostile groups. It's also not to say that the two situations are necessarily perfectly analogous. In fact, Sarah Palin's offense had minimal impact on her career, whereas Kathy Griffin's may have cost her hers (though I suspect Griffin's previous body of work had something to do with how quick people were to forget about her). Many people took opposite positions in the two situations due to factional hypocrisy. Others may have done so due to a legitimate analysis that the two situations were qualitatively different.

Herein lies an important side point. Rarely are two situations completely analogous, and, as any good appellate lawyer can tell you, two cases can always be distinguished. As a result, it can be difficult to tell if someone is taking seemingly opposite positions due to factional hypocrisy or simply because they feel that the two situations are different enough to warrant different positions. Worse still, people can cling to these differences, no matter how minor, to resolve any internal cognitive dissonance that would come with taking divergent positions. Thus, people not only justify their hypocrisy to others but also to themselves. Smart people never let facts or fairness get in the way of believing what they want to believe.

One last caveat here is about the use of hypotheticals. People will use hypotheticals, e.g., imagine if a (man/woman, Republican/Democrat, etc.) had (said/done) the same thing, as a way to show that other people are being inconsistent and unfair. There is nothing wrong with this method per se. However, there are a couple of problems with it in practice, the biggest one being that, since the hypothetical is, by definition, something that hasn't happened, there is no way of knowing how people would react. Thus, the hypothetical becomes what I call a Rorschach hypothetical, as people tend to project their own views and notions onto the hypothetical situation. It also ignores whether the original reaction is justified, as well as any qualitative differences the hypothetical situation may have from the real situation.

This is a little confusing in the abstract, so let's again look at a concrete example around which we can base our discussion. In 2017, comedienne Ellen DeGeneres tweeted, "Happy birthday, @KatyPerry! It's time to break out the big balloons!" referencing both Katy Perry's breasts and the lyrics of one of her songs.

Michael Rapaport, a guy who does something, somewhere, I guess, argued that had a guy tweeted the same thing, people would have lost their minds and the guy would have lost his career. That's the basic gist of the controversy—as much as I love and care about facts, the details here aren't all that important. I'm simply using this example to demonstrate why hypotheticals are bad.

First off, the biggest and most salient point is that no one knows how the public would have reacted had the same tweet been sent by a guy. The reaction Rapaport is attributing to the public is entirely in his mind, and probably says more about him and his assumptions about the world than it does about any objective reality. People, when dealing with these sorts of hypotheticals, tend to bring their own biases into the fray and project them onto the hypothetical situation. This makes the hypothetical unreliable and not very useful.

Furthermore, it ignores the fact that the situation itself may have been different had the tweet been sent by a man. A man talking about a woman's breasts is fundamentally different than a woman doing so. Finally, even if we grant that Mr. Rapaport's hypothetical would play out exactly as he imagined, the tweet referenced a Katy Perry song, and so the controversy surrounding his hypothetical man would have been a stupid controversy. It's not exactly a strong argument to say that we should be stupidly angry about something because we'd be stupidly angry about it if someone else had done it.

The way to promote consistency and ensure equal application of rights to all individuals is to take a procedural, rather than a substantive, view of what they are doing. Perhaps more clearly, this means to take a content-neutral view of things. Instead of Kathy Griffin holding Donald Trump's head, think of how you would react if a perfectly generic comedienne (so, Kathy Griffin) held the decapitated head of a generic world leader (definitely *not* Donald Trump). For another example, it's not any group protesting or rioting, it's simply people. Based solely on the actions at the protest, not the reason for the protest or the side the individuals were on, was it a protest, or did it cross the line to a riot?

This is easier said than done since we rarely consider our opinions outside of a real-world situation, and by the time we think of doing a rational, content-neutral analysis, we've already formed an emotional opinion that we are now trying to justify. Most people, whether they realize it or not, don't want to be fair, ensure the rights of others, or even listen to basic facts. They have their preconceived notions about the world, who and what is right and wrong, and will only accept information that either fits into those notions or can be twisted to do so. They will mercilessly attack anyone or anything that challenges these views.

If we, as a society, want to reap the benefits that Anglo-American society and its emphasis on individual rights bestow, we must overcome this instinct, allow people to express views across the entire political spectrum, and let the marketplace of ideas select the best among them. Ironically, there is no place in our society to say, "There is no place for this in our society," and use it to bully people and silence unpopular views. We must allow people to exhibit the natural deviation that humans possess, including ideologically, and not deny people their rights because they are ideological outliers. We must judge people on what they have actually done, not whether they or their ideas are popular. Entertaining ideas from across the ideological spectrum allows society to glean the best aspects of the diverse variety of human thought.

Unfortunately, though people may insist and truly believe

otherwise, it is not in human nature to value uniqueness and individuality. People want carbon copies of themselves. They want every other human being to conform to the ideological norm that they have established as being "right." Even people who insist that they love uniqueness and individuality do so only in the very narrow parameters their ego will allow. They may love racial or cultural diversity or embrace shallow displays of individual uniqueness such as quirky clothing or mannerisms. They may even tolerate opposing viewpoints on some issues that are, in reality, of minor importance to them. However, start challenging some of their core values or deeply held beliefs that are central to their self-identity, and you will quickly discover they are as intolerant as any other person.

It is no accident, then, that groups severely punish any deviation from cultural norms. This behavior persists to this day, both within society at large and within subsections of society. Take a look at how late-night talk show hosts responded to Jimmy Fallon having the audacity to interview a presidential candidate in 2016 (Donald Trump) or the treatment Tomi Lahren received from conservatives for revealing she's pro-choice. This isn't to say that these social repercussions are bad in and of themselves. In fact, they likely exist because enforcing a degree of homogeneity through norms and standards is necessary for group cohesion. However, they also have a chilling effect on individuals who do not fall within the acceptable range and prevent us from fully utilizing the variety of human deviation.

For this purpose, we developed due process. This procedural safeguard prevents individuals who hold unpopular views from being deprived of their rights by the voting majority without proper evidence and judicial review. And opportunistic politicians are prevented from exploiting the fear or unpopularity of segments of society to target those segments, as has generally happened in every society ever. In criminal cases, it prevents a version of mob justice by ensuring procedures that prevent someone from being punished because "everyone knows they did it" despite a lack of hard evidence. Though this system is far from perfect, it has generally served well.

Due process has served as an effective protection of individual rights from the government, and the government only. When individual rights are trampled on by private individuals and organizations, no such protection applies, nor should it. You may have the right to speak your mind, but I don't have to like it. And I have every right to decide that what you are saying is so deplorable that I don't want to associate with you, hire you, or publish what you're saying on whatever platform I have available. When you attempt to enforce due process on individuals and institutions, you get into a sticky area where protecting one individual's rights may trample on the rights of another. Though some states have used statutes to attempt to navigate this gray area, such as anti-discrimination laws that protect political views and civil suits for privacy violations, for the most part, people are on their own when it comes to private violations of rights. Similarly, companies and educational institutions are free to enact discipline with little to no evidence, if they choose to do so. Constitutional rights protect you from the government, not from private repercussions.

However, simply because individuals and institutions are not required to respect the same due process concerns as the government does not mean they should not respect due process. We do not have due process because we are required by the Constitution; we are required by the Constitution because it is the right thing to do. There are plenty of people who justify not using procedural safeguards in disciplinary hearings or disrespecting the rights of unpopular individuals, because due process protections don't apply and so they don't have to. This is the same "because I can" reasoning used by every bully in every schoolyard. Just because you don't have to do something doesn't mean it's not the right thing to do. I'm not arguing that every company needs to allow its employees to say racist things and keep their jobs or that educational institutions need the same "beyond a reasonable doubt" standard before passing discipline. I'm saying the same principles that led us to enshrine due process protections, both substantive and procedural, into our legal system should guide us in our private behavior.

Human beings exist across a wide spectrum in terms of thoughts, abilities, and values, and society thrives when we take advantage of this diversity. The advantage of the Anglo-American system of protecting individual rights and liberties is to allow each individual to exist and flourish wherever they fall rather than attempting to shoehorn and force people to exist on whatever narrow section of the bell curve we deem acceptable. Unfortunately, though human beings have an innate need to think of themselves as unique, one-of-a-kind individuals, they are not naturally willing to accept this behavior in others. In fact, it is because people are so attached to their view of self, including their oppositional self-definitions (i.e., I am who I am because I'm not X, or I don't tolerate X, etc.), that they feel the need to attack anyone who exhibits behaviors or traits they consider unacceptable. Agreeing to a set of rules and each individual complying with the agreed-upon rules allows us to take advantage of the individual deviation of human nature. Though we may not always do so perfectly, our respect for individual rights allows us to more peacefully coexist and contribute to the well-being of society.

CHAPTER 6

Rational Nationalism

What does it mean to be a Rational Nationalist? What policies should we support, and how should we conduct our day-to-day lives in pursuit of this ideal? Let's start with what a nationalist is, in general. To put it simply, a nationalist is a team player. It is someone who cares about the well-being of the group, is willing to make sacrifices for the group, puts the well-being of the group above their own, and behaves in the manner that will best help the group thrive. Although we generally think of nationalists as being based on racial, ethnic, or geographic groupings, in this construction of the word, one can be a nationalist with regards to any group to which they belong. All it means is that one's politics are designed to see the relevant group succeed over others. Really, it's about helping your team win.

When put this way, isn't everyone at their core a nationalist of some sort? After all, group interest is just an extended form of self-interest, and doesn't everyone want what's best for their communities? Kind of, but not necessarily. Everyone has some nationalist impulses; that is, some desire to see their group flourish over others and have a willingness to sacrifice and work to make that happen. The extent to which one exhibits these impulses exists on a continuum. In addition to the tug-of-war that comes with belonging to multiple groups with different, sometimes competing, interests, there are two other almost opposite forces that limit nationalism. These are selfishness and humanitarianism.

Selfishness is self-explanatory. It's putting one's self-interest above the welfare of the group or general good. We will use the term "utility" to refer to the benefit a group or individual gets from a course of action, and this utility will be assigned a higher score the greater the benefit. For example, the choice to either keep five dollars or give another person ten would be construed as keeping a utility of five for yourself or bestowing a utility of ten upon another. The reason we aren't just using dollars is that, for the most part, we'll be talking about the utility given to groups of people, and it's simpler to use utility to clearly demonstrate when the benefit to the group outweighs the benefit to oneself and by how much. It's akin to a common currency—a way to translate concrete and abstract benefits into the same terms so they can be compared more easily.

When given a choice between a course of action that will benefit himself X and one that will benefit the group X, a nationalist will choose the latter course of action, forgoing his own personal benefit to benefit the group an equal amount. The selfish person will take the utility of X to himself. This leads to the next point, which is that the tension between selfishness and nationalism, like most things, is not binary. It plays out on a scale. Very few people will be completely nationalist, willing to forgo any benefit to themselves, no matter how large, in exchange for any benefit to the group, no matter how small. Likewise, few people are completely selfish, willing to sacrifice nothing to benefit the group. The question for each individual is where their personal limits lie.

Some people, by nature, feel very little affinity for their groups, caring only for themselves. Some may acknowledge their defect (we are getting into the normative aspect of this work, so I feel comfortable terming it a defect, though the term is innately subjective), while others dismiss it under the guise of pseudo-intellectualism, but the end result is the same. Others, by contrast, are very nationalistic, willing to sacrifice a great deal to serve the greater interests of their groups. The best example is the soldier willing to sacrifice his or her life to defend their nation (or for whomever they are fighting).

The degree to which one is nationalistic can be devised with a simple test. We implied above that a neutral person would be indifferent between taking a benefit of X to themselves or bestowing it on their group. A nationalist would bestow it, whereas a selfish person would take it. How nationalistic or selfish a person is, is determined by how much the scales must be tipped to induce the individual to make the opposite choice. Does the benefit to the group have to be twice as much, or vice versa? The direction will determine whether the individual is nationalistic or selfish, and the factor will determine the degree. Note that while there is no innate judgment as to the morality of being selfish or nationalist and the terms are merely descriptive, I hope you can figure out my position.

However, there is another end of the spectrum: humanitarianism. An individual willing to give up a great deal of self-benefit may not be willing to do so because the benefit is going to their group, but simply because it is going to someone else. In other words, maybe they're just a giving person by nature. Without getting into the reasons why people may be altruistic in some or most circumstances, it is undeniable that there are people willing to sacrifice a great deal to benefit others, even when the other is not a group member.

We are going to call this humanitarianism, though our usage may differ slightly from the common vernacular, encompassing not just acts of aid but also a worldview that transcends narrow group loyalties. It is best described in the song "Imagine" by John Lennon. Essentially, this humanitarian perspective leads an individual to feel little or no attachment to their own specific groups, and no desire to see their groups prosper over others. However, this is because they feel an attachment, an affinity, and a willingness to work for the betterment of all mankind, rather than any specific subsection. In a sense, it is nationalism focused on the largest group of all: humanity. As such, unlike selfishness, it is not inherently incompatible with nationalist sentiment.

The degree to which you are willing to sacrifice for your group determines how much of a nationalist you are. The groups for which you are willing to sacrifice determine what kind of nationalist you are. People have multiple groups to which they belong, and the degree to which they identify with each group varies. My suspicion, which is based on nothing more than my intuition, is that most people who are nationalist will be nationalist with all their groups (in other words, they are simply team players by nature), though it is entirely possible for the degree of nationalism to vary dramatically from group to group. An individual could be completely nationalist to one group and completely selfish to another.

It is for this reason that humanitarianism and nationalism, at least insofar as we are using the terms, are not inherently contradictory. You are both a member of your nation and a member of humanity. It is entirely possible to want to see your group prosper, even relative to or over other groups, and still want to see humanity as a whole benefit. We are all loyal to multiple groups, and though these groups may have different interests, many times they are not mutually exclusive, and we are able to fully satisfy loyalties to all groups without harming the others.

Sometimes this is not possible, and when there is a direct conflict between the interests of two groups, which group you side with determines the degree of your relative nationalism. The test here is essentially the same as for determining nationalism versus selfishness, except here the benefit is to one of two groups rather than yourself. Take, as an example, humanitarianism versus nationalism. If given the choice between a benefit of X to all of humanity, or the same benefit applied specifically to one's group, the humanitarian would choose the former and the nationalist, the latter. The degree to which the scales must be tipped to induce the opposite decision determines your relative nationalism between the two groups (remembering that humanitarianism is humanity-based nationalism). The same test can be applied to any two groups to which an individual belongs. Though this construct of "nationalism" can be applied to any group identity, it most commonly applies to one's nation or country.

Rational refers to the ability to put our emotions aside and use intelligent analysis to decide strategically what is best for our country. What, then, is the best approach to serve the cause of Rational Nationalism? In a very general sense, we need to be strategic and rational in our approach and policies. Nationalism can be our motivating emotion, but we must be able to set our emotions aside and think about what will best strengthen our

nation. Too often, people in general, and nationalists specifically, allow their emotions to cloud their judgment, reacting and
forming knee-jerk opinions rather than strategic ones. Though
their hearts are in the right place, our strength as a species comes
from our ability to think strategically. We must be able to put
emotions aside to do what's necessary and best, even as love for
our country remains our motivation.

Our primary goal should be to strengthen our nation on the
world stage. We do this not only by having the strongest military and the strongest economy but by fully capitalizing on the
soft power of our ideas and ensuring that we as a nation are
fully mobilized. To achieve this, we must rely on sound, rational
principles rather than engaging in gut reactions; we must make
use of our full intellectual and scientific capacities. We must, for
example, base our economic policies around economic laws and
principles, rather than falling prey to simplistic arguments and
political demagoguery.

This is what is meant by "Rational Nationalism." It is still
nationalism, but without the emotionally reactive opposition to
things like trade or immigration, or the instinctive isolationism.
It possesses the fire of nationalism but applies those goals with a
cooler head. We use our intellectual capacity and scientific principles to determine the best course and the best policies to augment
the power of our nation. Our goal, however, is to strengthen our
nation to the furthest extent possible, determining our policies
based on what is good for the country as a unit, rather than squab-
bling over who gets what or what is good for certain segments
of the nation. It is a complete and violent rejection of internally
divisive, one-group-against-the-other domestic politics.

At the end of the day, all policy becomes foreign policy. Our focus is the status of our nation amongst the nations of the world. Given that our place in the world is determined by the strength of our economy and our military, our focus ought to be on expanding these two elements as much as possible. Everything else is secondary to serving the greater purpose of national strength.

Since we are focused on our place on the world stage, our concern must be with relative, rather than absolute, gains. It does not matter how strong we are; it matters how much stronger we are than everyone else. This concept runs into more opposition with regard to economic policy than military policy, so that is what I will focus the conversation on. With trade, our concern is getting more benefit, or at least as much, than with whomever we are trading. If we are to harm our economy to protect the environment, we must make sure that it is done in a multilateral way so that we don't fall behind other nations economically.

The concept becomes extremely complicated when applied to real-world situations because of the number of players and factors to consider, but it should remain the guiding principle. For example, when dealing with a much smaller, weaker nation, we can be much laxer in the relative gains of any bilateral trade deal. Even if they will benefit twice as much as we will, that is probably still acceptable to us, since they are not going to become a rival in terms of overall strength, and we will still benefit relative to all nations not involved in the deal. When dealing with a nation such as China, which is much closer in terms of overall strength, we must be more defensive of our relative gains. The complicated nature of real-world politics means that there will not always be a clear-cut answer as to our optimal strategy as a nation. This can lead to disagreement, and we will address how to resolve these disagreements at the end of this section.

There is another important caveat on trade, which is that it would be a mistake to look at trade relations through a purely economic prism. Sometimes, the purpose of trade isn't economic, but geopolitical. We may want to accept trade deals that, though not great for us from an economic perspective, serve other purposes, such as strengthening our allies' economies or enhancing our influence within a partner nation. These goals may justify accepting trade deals that give our partners greater economic benefit than we receive.

Though the military and the economy are the two most important manifestations of global power, and we should attempt to maximize our military and economic potential, we should not be so quick to discount the soft power of our culture and ideas. We discussed above how respecting individual rights has allowed us to maximize our human capital, taking full advantage of the talents and ingenuity of our populace. However, individual rights also have a universal appeal, as does democracy. By standing up and defending these principles, we can influence people across the world to cooperate with our agenda, not because they need to, but because they want to. This concept is very deeply related to the idea of American exceptionalism.

In order for this to be effective on the world stage, however, we have to actually have a policy of standing up for our principles. Sometimes, this means putting principle above self-interest. If, for example, we want the world's cooperation in fighting terrorism, then we have to make it clear that we are the good guys. This might mean acting like it even when it isn't directly the best policy; for example, by closing Guantanamo. Exercising soft power requires caring about how things are viewed by others.

Respecting individual rights also helps to keep a united population, and it is easier for a nation to project its power on the world stage when it has domestic peace. We have seen multiple examples of powerful nations torn apart by domestic strife. One of the historic strengths of the Anglo-American nations has been a lack of fighting within our own populations (that isn't to say it hasn't occurred, just that it hasn't been as destructive as elsewhere). People are more likely to obey and follow a government they view as legitimate, just, and predictable, and are less likely to revolt.

Respecting individual rights keeps us acting as one whole nation, instead of wasting time and resources putting down domestic uprisings and fighting amongst ourselves. Respect for individual rights adds to the legitimacy and justice with which our government is viewed by the population, and the rule of law and due process prevent the arbitrary abuse of power that would encourage individual citizens to protect themselves. It also provides an outlet for grievances to be expressed, rather than being bottled up until they boil over, and elections provide a certain responsiveness short of taking up arms or full-fledged rebellion. That isn't to say these mechanisms always work perfectly or leave everyone satisfied; it is simply to reinforce the idea that they are a key part of our strength.

This is why it is so important to respect disagreements and resolve them through agreed-upon mechanisms. These mechanisms constitute a key feature of Anglo-American strength and longevity, and once people start to ignore or go around the prescribed methods of dispute resolution, it causes a breakdown in the system that leads to us fighting each other. Furthermore, as mentioned above, there will be disagreements even among people with the same goals. It serves no purpose for us to tear each other apart when, ultimately, we are trying to achieve the same thing.

There is a notable caveat to this seemingly utopian vision of tolerance, however. This tolerance is only extended so far as people actually have the same motives. There are those among us who do not seek to do what's best for their country. They serve a selfish, humanitarian, or other ideological agenda rather than pursuing the well-being of their nation. Perhaps they only care about a segment of the population, willing to benefit that segment at the cost of the well-being of the nation as a whole. For these people, no tolerance is necessary. We cannot resolve disagreements peacefully through rational debate and democratic mechanisms when, at the end of the day, we are serving different masters.

AGENDA FOR RATIONAL NATIONALISM

It is all well and good to discuss in utopian terms how we ought to come together to use empirical evidence to develop policies that advance our agenda and resolve disagreements with rational discourse, but life is messier on the ground than in the ivory tower. A philosophy is not complete without a concrete agenda for advancing its cause. As you can imagine, the policy positions I envision for Rational Nationalism are fairly open-ended, using empirical evidence and rationality to develop the best policies to strengthen our respective nations. They are more focused on the ends than the means, tolerating a wide range of political positions and views so long as they are taken in good faith with an eye toward fortifying the strength of our nation as opposed to benefiting a specific subsection at the cost of the whole.

Nevertheless, the line must be drawn somewhere, and there is a core set of concepts that defines a Rational Nationalist. First, you must put the well-being of the nation above all, forming your politics for the benefit of the general welfare even if it's to your individual disadvantage. This means not prioritizing the well-being of any political party, union, oneself, or any other group above the well-being of the nation. We can disagree strategically, but it is not possible to be a nationalist if you are not putting the nation first. This means, for example, not looking out for American businesses or American workers, but for the American economy. Second, there is a core platform that should be the focus of a rational, nationalist agenda. That platform is domestic peace, prosperity, and power.

Domestic peace is similar to the idea of law and order, though to think of it simply in those terms is a lazy mischaracterization. In reality, it is closer to a combination of law and order and social justice. It rests on the idea that for a people to be strong, they must be united. If people are too busy fighting amongst themselves, either figuratively or literally, their ability to mobilize and achieve any sort of common goal will be greatly diminished or eliminated. Thus, we cannot tolerate any sort of unrest, domestic terrorism, or civil disorder. The law must be respected and obeyed, and those who violate it must be punished.

However, this does not necessarily require a repressive, heavy-handed approach. People are more likely to follow laws that they respect and perceive as fair. Part of the reason for the historical success of the Anglo-American nations is our criminal justice system and the fact that our societies are generally seen as being just by their members. Where unrest is caused by legitimate complaints about injustices, we are better off addressing these injustices than attempting to coerce compliance by sheer force. There is no reason to rely on force to gain domestic peace when it can be achieved by reasonable legal reforms.

Similarly, demanding domestic peace is different from not tolerating dissent. One of the most fundamental rights is the right to disagree with government or society, and the right to express this disagreement. No matter what the government or society does, the diversity of human thought means that somebody somewhere will have a grievance with it. Allowing these grievances to be expressed through peaceful, legal means provides a meaningful, healthy release that prevents these grievances from boiling over into revolt. As long as the dissent is within legal confines, it is perfectly acceptable for dissent to be expressed, and we should welcome it.

The flip side of this is that when the law is broken, it must be punished. We as a society must decide where the line is, and when the line is crossed, we must act accordingly. There can be no excuses as to the law being unjust or the punishment being too harsh. If either of these is the case, the law or the punishment should be changed. However, once we have decided where the line is and how crossing it must be punished, we must be consistent and strong in doing so. There is a great deal of room for disagreement on how to change the law and punish violators. Once made, the law must be enforced efficiently and effectively and respected by all, with no exceptions.

The next is economic prosperity. Economic prosperity basically means maximizing economic growth. There may be less room for disagreement on how to achieve this than with domestic peace. We have an entire field of economics dedicated to studying how to go about this, and we ought to defer to the experts in evaluating the economic impact of our policies. Yes, there are some areas where even the experts may disagree, but we should follow evidence-based expertise as far as it can take us. Even if the experts don't know everything, they know a lot more than the elected politicians who would be wise to heed their advice.

At first, this seems like an obvious, uncontroversial policy position. After all, who would oppose growing the economy? A lot of people for a lot of reasons, as it turns out. The issue lies in the trade-offs that must be made in the real world to support economic growth. All economic growth means is that the economy, taken as a whole, will become larger, generating more wealth for the whole nation. It says nothing about which areas of the country will grow, which segments of the population or sectors of the economy will benefit, or how the newly generated wealth will be distributed. If I asked people if they wanted more economic growth, everyone would say yes. If I asked whether they would rather see 4 percent growth distributed evenly throughout the economy, or 5 percent economic growth that would go exclusively to the already wealthy, the answers would be quite different. The reality is somewhere between these two extremes, but the choices reflected in policy more closely resemble the latter.

The point here is that since we are trying to strengthen our nation as a whole, we are going to tend to support whatever policies lead to the greatest growth overall as opposed to trying to dictate economic winners and losers. This isn't to say we are going to be completely blind to the economic struggles of our people. It merely recognizes that wars are won with gold and that economic power, particularly in this day and age, is arguably the most important factor in a nation's influence on the global stage. Economic strength funds our military and was largely responsible for our victories in both World War II and the Cold War. If we desire to maximize our strength, economic concerns are central to this goal.

Economic growth is simply a framework from which to start

discussing economic policy, and we must only rely on experts for guidance on how to achieve this. This doesn't mean we can't deviate and disagree about the extent on which we balance economic growth with achieving other goals. In fact, sometimes we may have to decide between economic growth and one of the other two pillars of Rational Nationalism: domestic peace or power. Too much income inequality can threaten domestic unity, and sometimes it may be in our interest to sacrifice our economic interest to achieve a military or diplomatic objective. However, at its core, a nationalist must prioritize the economic health of their nation over their own economic interests.

The final pillar of Rational Nationalism is power. Power is the only true goal of nationalism. The attainment of power is the only true goal of politics. Everything else is a means to achieve this end. Power is, simply defined, the ability to impact change and control outcomes. When we are referring to the relationship between nations, power has traditionally been about the ability to control land and resources. Today, the ability to shape and enforce global norms of behavior has gained importance.

As evolved as the Western world likes to think it has become, at the end of the day, all power derives from military power. As much as diplomatic, economic, and other forms of peaceful dispute resolution are in vogue, when push comes to shove, the nation with the biggest guns is still going to win. As such, it is completely necessary and appropriate for us to do all we can to ensure our military is the best equipped, the best prepared, and the most effective fighting force in the world. Military preparedness must always be our number one priority. Though this does not mean tolerating wasteful or excessive spending on the military, it does mean that we must be willing to give our fighting men and women everything they need to do their jobs.

Military power, in turn, is derived from economic power, and herein lies the greatest trade-off we face when setting budgetary priorities. In the short term, military power reigns supreme. However, over longer periods of time, economic power is what allows military power to be augmented or maintained. World War II is a prime example of this. Germany had greater military strength, at least in the beginning, which is why the early stages of the war were marked by German victory and advancement. However, the greater natural resources of the Allies meant that, over time, they were able to sustain their effort in a way the Germans could not. Thus, it was largely economic strength as opposed to military strength that ultimately led to Allied victory.

The point of all this is that, when we are not faced with an immediate military threat, it may be justifiable to focus more on building a strong economic base of power rather than building an immediately effective military. These are not mutually exclusive goals. We should build our economy at the same time we maintain the world's most powerful fighting force. However, when deciding whether to invest in economic development or military development, it is necessary to weigh the costs and benefits of both.

There is another benefit to economic power that considers a reality the discussion up to this point has ignored: it is no longer as acceptable, at least among Western nations, to use military force. We no longer live in an age where it's acceptable to simply take what you want, though the degree to which this is true is debatable, as Russia has shown in recent years in Ukraine and Crimea. Couple this with the fact that the cost of a potential nuclear war makes conflicts between nuclear powers highly unattractive, and you are left with the conclusion: economic influence is often a more effective means of achieving a desired end than military force.

Economic power can work as either a carrot or a stick and is most effective when wielded in conjunction with other nations, which is a natural lead-in to discuss soft, or diplomatic, power. Soft power is the ability to persuade other actors, either nations or groups within nations, to go along with your agenda. This allows you to augment your strength by combining it with that of others, or to achieve your goals without having to rely on force. This can be achieved by persuasion or coercion and is particularly necessary with issues such as civil wars or terrorism, where we need people to act a certain way. We can kill our enemies easily enough, but we can't make them do anything they don't want to do.

This leads us to seek answers to the questions we should always be asking: What's the point? Why do we want or need to obtain all this power? For all of human history outside of the past three-quarters of a century, power has been about the ability to control land and resources. Whether we are beyond that or not is debatable, but we have seen a noted difference in the international order since the end of the Second World War under American leadership. Now, the purpose of the power we seek is not to control land or resources but to shape the world we live in.

This brings us back to one of our themes. Just because we seek power does not mean there must be anything aggressive or malicious behind it. It is better for us to exercise benevolent power. In the same way that we can achieve domestic peace by ensuring that the law is just, we can better get nations and actors to accept our leadership by making sure it is in their best interest to do so. This may seem overly idealistic, and in some cases may be impossible, but by pushing for a peaceful, predictable, and fair international order, we can gain the cooperation of the rest of the world, or large elements thereof, in achieving our objectives.

SOURCES OF POLICY DISAGREEMENT REGARDING THE AGENDA

All nationalism boils down to is patriotism. We recognize that life is a team sport, and we are openly and unapologetically playing for our team. The best way to help said team may be open for debate. Even those who agree with most or all of what has been written here may have some dramatic differences when it comes time to shape and formulate policy. Here are a few sources of disagreement that can be found within the philosophical framework put forth.

The first source is the relative weight that one puts on situational versus ideological explanations for Anglo-American success. As discussed previously, Britain became the greatest empire the world has ever seen. It only left its hegemonic seat when it was replaced by the United States, a country with which it shares its history, culture, and ideals. Is it those ideals that led to the dominance of Anglo-American nations? Or is it merely a coincidence that Britain and the United States rose to the pinnacle of world power one after another?

The answer to this question may have serious implications as to how willing we are to deviate from the norms set forth. If the reason that the Anglo-American people have become great is our philosophy—that is, our respect for democratic norms, individual rights, and free market economics—then it makes sense that we would continue to ride the horse that got us here. We should ensure the protection of those ideals, even where it looks like these ideals may weaken or work against our immediate interests. We must have faith that, over time, our respect for Anglo-American philosophy will lead to our success and our victory.

If, however, Anglo-American success can be attributed to situational factors such as geography, then there is no magic behind our philosophy. The cultural norms are merely coincidental, and we would have flourished whether we'd chosen free-market democracy, communism, fascism, or any other form of governance. Attributing Anglo-American success to historical coincidence rather than cultural aspects opens a much broader range of the political spectrum. Someone attributing our success to philosophical causes would have to operate within the box of Anglo-American, pro-democratic norms. If there is nothing special about these norms, there is no reason not to embrace the extremes of the political spectrum should one believe that these extremes would strengthen their nation.

Of course, as with most things, this is not an all-or-nothing proposition. In all likelihood, both philosophical and situational factors led to the success of the Anglo-American people. The point here is simply to say that the relative weight we give to philosophical factors in affecting the success of the Anglo-American people will influence the way we approach policymaking. Faith in Anglo-American philosophy is likely to be a moderating influence, leading one to be more skeptical of radical or extreme solutions.

Another potential source of discord is the degree to which one chooses to embrace factional versus transactional politics. In essence, all politics is transactional. There is no such thing as an enemy or an ally in absolute terms. There are only interests. Allies are merely those with shared interests; enemies are those with opposing interests. As interests shift, so do alliances. History is full of allies who became enemies and enemies who became allies as the political winds shifted. This also applies quite clearly within our domestic politics.

Theoretically, the only interest we should be serving is the best interests of the United States (using American politics as an example). We should all vote for and support the policies that will best support the United States, whether we think those policies are put forth by the Republican or the Democratic Party. There should be no hesitancy on the part of a Republican to vote with the Democrats when they think the Democrats are right on the issue, or vice versa. Yet, we've seen our nation become heavily factional, with people forming their opinions based on party allegiance rather than deciding party allegiance based on their opinions. This is completely backward from the way things should be.

However, though the interest of the United States must always come first, a degree of factionalism may be necessary or proper. We would be blind if we argued that either party purely served the interests of the United States. Sure, some members of both parties are motivated by what's best for their country, but many are predominantly looking out for the interests of specific groups or subsections of the population, whether they be ideologues, donors, religious folks, labor unions, corporations, or so on. Regardless of their motivation, both parties put forth a platform of ideas, some of which may help the United States and some of which may harm it. If one were to believe the platform of one party was far superior to that of the other for the well-being of the United States, they might side with that party and work for its electoral success, even if there are some areas where they believe the party to be wrong. This is because the benefit of having their preferred party in power outweighs the cost of tolerating a policy they think is poor. It is a strategic form of nationalism, putting the overall interest of the nation first by ensuring the party best equipped for its prosperity prevails.

Again, this is not an all-or-nothing proposition. Though none of us should have any loyalty to either party, instead viewing each party as mere tools to work toward our goals, it will ultimately be necessary to choose one over the other. The degree of partisanship in this country at this time is completely unacceptable and should not be tolerated. However, there is nothing wrong with making a judgment call that one party is superior to the other, so long as your primary loyalty is to the nation.

There is one more key element we have to be wary of in the pursuit of Rational Nationalism. Nationalism, being based on group identity and emotion, often embodies an "us vs. them" mentality. At its core, there is nothing wrong with this. Politics is a team sport, and there is nothing wrong with unabashedly going all in for your team. I respect and admire the passionate patriotism of people so dedicated to their nation. However, since such politics are based on passion, they can often lead to a reactive, knee-jerk rejection of "them" in favor of "us," even in cases where such a reaction may go against the best interest of the nation. We see this form of nationalism manifest today in the United States, Britain, and across Europe, and it generally takes the form of vehement opposition to both trade and immigration.

In reality, both trade and immigration are complex issues that require a strategic approach rather than wholesale rejection or acceptance. When done correctly, trade and immigration can have a great benefit to the nation, helping to grow the economy and gain a competitive edge over rival nations. However, too many people are willing to simplify the issue as trade is good or bad, either embracing all trade deals and all immigration (legal or illegal) or rejecting all trade deals and all immigration. Sometimes, this is done to manifest their respective humanitarian or nationalist ideals, and sometimes it is due to the fact that it is simpler to be pro- or anti-something than to address the complexities of the issue. Either way, when we forgo potential gains for ideological reasons, our nation loses.

My point is not to take any specific position on either trade or immigration, but to point out that, since we are motivated by patriotism, we run the risk of allowing our emotions to get the better of us. We need to have hot hearts but cool heads. We should absolutely be passionate about our nation and allow love for our nation to motivate us to do everything we can for the benefit of the nation, but we must be smart in how we go about it. We must be disciplined and strategic. Doing what is best for our nation, even when it's not what we want, is the truest form of patriotism.

This concludes our discussion of what I consider to be a relatively unique take on nationalism. In essence, nationalism is the recognition that life generally and politics specifically are team sports that require the willingness to fully and unabashedly play for your team. Here, we have often referred to this as Rational Nationalism. The argument of Rational Nationalism is that you pursue the well-being of your team in the most strategic manner possible.

In addition to informing our politics, this philosophy has implications for our daily lives. We ought to maximize our own personal health and growth, both on a physical and an intellectual level. This means making decisions and undertaking pursuits that lead to our personal edification as a patriotic calling in order to maximize our potential. In the same way that a team succeeds based on how hard its individual players train, so too do nations prosper based on the health and devotion of their populations. It is not enough to want to see our nation thrive; we, as individuals, must take the steps and make the sacrifices necessary for it to do so.

This means that every decision must be made based on the benefit to the group you are trying to serve and without the biases of your personal desires. There is nothing wrong with the pursuit of self-interest, per se. Much of our economic success has come from the innovation of individuals pursuing their self-interests. However, we must make sure that our pursuit of self-interest coincides with the general good, or at least does it no harm. In the same way, there is nothing wrong with hedonism or excessive consumption, per se. It becomes an issue when the pursuit of hedonistic callings makes us soft and less capable of serving our nation or causes externalities that impact the general good. The success of the group must always be our primary call.

Human beings are to society what a cell is to the human body. Ultimately, we are insignificant. We die quickly, leave no lasting notion of us as individuals, and are easily replaced by thousands of other identical units serving the exact same purpose. However, by remaining healthy and performing our role to the best of our abilities—by acting as Rational Nationalists—we can be part of something greater than ourselves, something that will survive long after we are gone and forgotten. Ensuring the survival of our groups is the highest calling. It is the primary purpose of our existence.

About the Author

Lee Ellis was born in Pittsburgh, PA. He graduated from Notre Dame High School in Elmira, NY, in 2004 and graduated summa cum laude from the University of Pittsburgh in 2008 with a dual-major in Political Science and Psychology, with a minor in Economics.